Forget Having Kids. I'm Having Fun

1000 Random Reasons
I Chose To Be #Childfree

Also by Dane Reid

Dana The Procrastinator

Dana is a boy who lives in a big city, but the fast paced city spirit does not live in Dana. When Dana's constant procrastination causes him to miss out on his own surprise birthday party, Dana turns over a new leaf. This story will help your children realize the value of time and opens up the opportunity for discussion between children and adults about time management. www.KidsReid.com

Forget Having Kids. I'm Having Fun

1000 Random Reasons
I Chose To Be #Childfree

Dane A. Reid

Published by
Dane Reid Media LLC

Library of Congress Control Number: 2022918010
ISBN: 979-8-218-03275-3

Reid, Dane A.

Forget Having Kids. I'm Having Fun:
1000 Random Reasons I Chose To Be #Childfree

PRINTED IN THE UNITED STATES OF AMERICA

Table of Contents

Forward
By Dr. Mara Karpel

The decision about whether or not to have children is a very private and personal one—or it should be. Taking on the responsibility to raise a human in such a time as the one we are living ought to be thought out carefully and with seriousness so the children brought into this world are wanted, loved, and cared for. It would also behoove us to make the decision about whether parenthood is the right path for our own purposeful life. After all, not everyone is cut out for parenting. And living a passionate life rarely comes about by following the path that we are told by society we are supposed to take.

Dane has made the decision to never father any children, even going through the medical procedure to assure that he does not procreate. And he gives us a number of reasons why he has made that decision. It's very fitting that the numbers he's assigned for each of his reasons are random and not in any sequence. The fact is that he doesn't have to tell us any of his reasons at all. He could just say, "This is my life, and I will follow the path that's right for me."

As someone who has not had children of my own, I know the urge to give explanations and assurances of our love for children, because we've made the choice to not bring any new ones into the world. For me, as a woman, the pressure was intense during childbearing years. I was criticized by all sorts of people consisting of complete strangers and even my own doctor. My choice to not become a mother was obviously going against the grain and was highly resented by people whom I don't even know in society.

As Dane writes, "A growing number of people who love children don't want to be parents, but we still have so much to offer in supporting the growth of children." We are all needed to grow the children of our communities, even if we haven't birthed them because, as it's said, "It takes a village."

Reading Dane's experience, one of making that same decision I did, but from the perspective of a man, learning about the pressures he's also faced because of his decision, has been an eye-opening story. And it's a very timely one at this particular time in our history. When we're able to choose our own authentic life, we are free to live a life of passion and to have sincere compassion and generosity for others, to create kinder communities and a kinder world. It makes us better able to be a powerful member of the village and help create environments where our children feel wanted and encouraged to live with joy and vitality.

Dane's writing is engaging and entertaining. His message is profound. When we look at what he's expressed from the lens of authenticity, we will witness a human being daring to make personal choices that are not based on expectations, but on what is the best path for himself. His example is an invitation to all of us to live our passion and to be fully present. Only then will we be free to live our purpose and become vital and caring members of our world community.

Dr. Mara Karpel is a psychologist, author of The Passionate Life: Creating Vitality; Joy At Any Age, host of Blog Talk Radio show, Dr. Mara Karpel & Your Golden Years, and contributing writer to several publications, including Huffington Post, Thrive Global, and Sivana East.

www.DrMaraKarpel.com

Dedications and Thanks

This book is dedicated to parents, especially my parents, who understood the difficulty in raising sons and put a hundred percent of themselves into loving, educating, and setting great examples for us. No parent is perfect, but mine are loving parents who could've authored a book on raising boys into successful men. Education was everything to them. My mother painstakingly taught me to read before I started school. I didn't make it easy on her.

I also dedicate this book to my uncles and aunts who were my village that helped me become who I am. And I salute my four brothers who are all loving fathers. My brother Dez taught me much of what I knew about life, and he loved writing creative stories. Wanting to be like him, I picked up a pen and paper and wrote chapters of stories starting in first grade. I also especially honor my brother Julian who loved his daughter Isabella with all of his heart and spoke about her every day until his last. Julian was one of my best friends and travel buddy and often joked about my escapades. He died of a broken heart, but I keep him in mine everywhere I go.

Being a parent is the hardest job on the planet, yet no one needs a license or pre-screening to become one. This book is dedicated to those who pre-screened themselves. It's dedicated to the child-free community. To those who recognize that having children is more than giving birth. It's dedicated to the people who understand that having children is a huge undertaking that is not for them. You know yourself. You've looked at the world. You've studied the evidence and done what's best for you and any child you might've had. Sometimes the responsible decision isn't the popular one. The path to happiness is more difficult than the road to acceptance.

Finally, I dedicate this book to everyone who has had to make difficult parenting decisions, including financial ones, and to those who are simply trying to carve out a good life for themselves.

Preface

This book is about my road to happiness. It's about self-love and self-care. It's about healing. It's about forgiving myself for my mistakes and the pain I've caused others. It's about forgiving the mistakes of others. This book is about planning and preventing missteps.

Raising children today is very different than when I was growing up. Our modern world pays closer attention to mental health, depression, suicide, and figuring out where we fit in life. I grew up in a time when "toughing it out" was the only way. I still believe in toughing things out but also see great value in mental health awareness and knowing oneself and one's limits. I try to strike a balance between those two elements in this book and in my life, which have at times seemed at odds.

There is a difference between being child-free and being a child hater. This book is both for the people who don't know the difference and for people who do. I spent years helping to educate children, and I loved it. I have the greatest nieces and nephews on the planet, and I love them all, and I'm so proud of them. And I'll never forget the joy I witnessed doing book signings for my children's book, *Dana the Procrastinator*. A growing number of people who love children don't want to be parents, but we still have so much to offer in supporting children's growth. Our society, too, needs to grow in its understanding. If someone says they don't want to be a parent, accept it and leave them in peace.

Note: this book challenges traditional ideas of a man's role in deciding whether or not to have children and how that affects his life, the child's life, and the mother's life. It features stories that highlight the difficulties faced when only one person has the right to decide and the desperation sometimes felt when that person holds the keys to both of your futures.

In an era when women's bodies and reproductive rights are being legislated and adjudicated, it's more important than ever that men pick up the slack. I'm not telling men not to have kids. I'm telling men not to have more kids than they can care for. I'm advocating exercising the few options we have to prevent the birth of children we may not want.

So here's my message to men: Have as many children as you are willing to be a father to and no more. The power is in your pants. Also? Vasectomies don't hinder your abilities.

Introduction

Growing up is hard to do. When I was a kid, I couldn't wait to be an adult. I imagined this life where I was rich through osmosis, and all I did was watch cartoons all day from the comfort of my bed.

As I got older and crossed the threshold of adulthood, I realized that all those days in school where my scheduled actions were dictated to me were just dress rehearsals for the real show. Adulthood would be ruthless, and if I thought expectations would disappear just because I didn't have a teacher or parents telling me what to do, I had a rude awakening waiting. Not only did I have to navigate the waters of bill paying, job working, and more bill paying, society still had expectations of adulthood for me.

Society said that once I graduated, I was expected to find a good job, buy a nice car, get a house, find a partner, marry her, and then have 2.5 children. I thought reaching the magical age of 18 meant that I had no more pressure. Instead, 18 and the years that followed meant new and more intense pressures. Childhood was just training camp.

I watched many of my friends follow the pattern that adulthood set for them. They finished college and got good professional jobs. *Check*. They bought their dream cars. *Check*. They purchased houses or leased nice apartments or condos. *Check*. They found partners. *Check*. And they had children. Mission accomplished. I resisted those things. One friend called me Benjamin Button. I didn't want to be a *grown-up* grown-up. I just wanted to be kinda grown-up.

In the early 2010's I saw friends who, like me had resisted adulthood, collapse under the weight of inevitability. They had children, which seemed strange because, like me, they were still so young. Others traded their insouciant dating days for stability. My network of like-minded friends was crumbling. Friends who once encouraged me to run into the fire of indiscretion became the pillars of measured advice. Whenever life is moving forward while you are stuck in place, it's like you're moving in reverse.

I had fallen behind in this race called adulthood. I was just as capable as my peers, but I had made few steps towards proving it. It was time to take substantive action. I began to desire one partner that I could build a life with. I wanted good credit and I had already taken steps to successfully grow my voiceover business. I wanted a home like my friends had and to have adult conversations about investments. I wanted to talk about hundreds of thousands of dollars instead of merely hundreds. I envied them in all but one way: My friends liked talking about their kids.

I had no desire to be a parent. And as I delved deeper into their conversations, I learned that parenthood came with more disadvantages than advantages. My friends mostly said that it was worth the disadvantages to reap the benefits, but when I would ask them to quantify it, they weren't able to. I need metrics, and without a chart, I can't see the benefit of investing. Over the years, our conversations became more candid about how hard they had to work, how much their kids misbehaved, and other challenges of parenthood. Some even regretted their decisions to be parents. My single mother friends complained about needing more support, and my single father friends griped about conflicts with the mothers of their children. To top things off, parenthood was non-refundable and non-transferable. None of this seemed fruitful to me.

So, whenever my friends told me their parenting horror stories (and there were many), I would respond, "That's why I never wanted kids." I started to randomly number the reasons I opted out of parenthood. It got to a point where my friends started numbering the reasons for me. That running joke ran so long that I started writing everything down. After years of keeping notes, I was encouraged by a friend to compile my collection of reasons into a book. I contemplated it, researched books about being childfree written by men, then, after facing the many fears associated with writing a book, decided to do it.

But you know that already. After all, you're holding that book in your hands.

Chapter 1
The Vas Deferens

I could smell the stench of burning flesh. *My* burning flesh. How did I end up here, lying with my legs open on a chair where 20,000 men had been before me? No, I'm not a man-hooker. I'm doing something millions of brave guys from all around the world have done. They were brave pioneers. But me? I wasn't so brave. I was there with a doctor who was burning away my fears. The fears I had since I began having sex in my mid-teens. Maybe even before. He was burning away years of bad experiences, tough decisions, and insecurities about money and the fear that I would be caught in a situation for which there was no turning back. I was slamming the door shut on being one of those guys who wished that one night hadn't happened, all while simultaneously confronting the fear that many men have when getting a vasectomy: would I ever again have any glorious nights?

While my pragmatic self knew this was the smartest decision I had ever made, I couldn't help but feel a sense of sadness. My entire life, I avoided making decisions that I could not change and might someday regret, and here I was making one of those decisions. While not impossible, undoing a vasectomy isn't as simple as drawing a reverse card in Uno. Even if you pay the estimated 10k to get your man juices reset to factory condition, there is no guarantee it will work. And 10k is a lot more cash than the $600 I spent on this vas deferens dividing experience. Regardless of any future regret, I was here, and I wasn't going to leave the table mid-flesh-melt. I had thought about doing this for too long, researched this too hard, and was ready.

Kinda.

Before I arrived at my appointment, I prepped myself for the possibility that I would be denied the chance to even get this procedure done. The internet had me shaken, thinking that the doctor would turn me away. I had read horror stories of doctors refusing to tie the tubes of women with no children. I was prepared with my story for when the doctor asked if I had children. And he did. I told him I had none, and then he mumbled some words like, "Okay, you just decided that wasn't for you," and then instructed me to pull my pants down. The double standard is real. I had the right as a man not to have children, but my female counterparts had to make the decision in full consultation with their doctors. Still, I pressed forward, embracing my advantage.

I can't begin to imagine the pressure women face in these scenarios. From early on, they are given baby dolls and have it consciously and unconsciously instilled in them that having children is their destiny. I understand that pressure only to a degree. As a man, I am expected to fulfill my legacy, whatever that means. At least, that's how it's presented to me. I don't think it's dictated to women the same way. Men can produce from puberty to death and even beyond. Apparently, thanks to science and a possible touch of rigor mortis, the squirter never stops squirting, even after our brain stops working (MacKinnon, 2022). One could even argue that our brains stop working before and during sex, but I digress. Men are endowed with this lifelong superpower to turn the pipes on at any time, and the fact that I was turning them off permanently went against the universe's design.

I never really believed that design. I have always rejected the word "should" as an incredibly subjective word created to make everyone into thoughtless robots. (They should get rid of that word.) I didn't want to "should have kids." For much of my adult life, I felt like I had to defend my choice not to "should" be a father. People simply don't reject the "should" of parenthood. People have children, and that's it. No questions asked. And whenever someone decides not to, it's like they are a weirdo, or a contrarian, or worse, a threat to society. People, especially those who claim to have made the best decision of their lives, often harbor hatred toward those who have decided not to. I never understood it. It's the dad you just met in line at McDonald's telling his kid they can't get two toys in their happy meal who is most angered when he finds out that you ordered a number 5 for yourself. And while those kinds of people bear the brunt of the anger, they are not the only ones who seem upset by your very personal decision.

Upsetting others played a part in why I didn't have a vasectomy years earlier. I never wanted to turn off the women I dated. At one point, I was dating someone seriously for five years. The relationship seemed great, and she had convinced me that we should have at least one child together. We fantasized and even named our imaginary future daughter "Summer." Heck, I was the one who came up with the name. I was all in on this dream because I loved her. But when the relationship ended, I realized it was not what I really wanted. That was *her* dream. I wanted peace. I wanted freedom. But I didn't want to tell her that for fear that it would ruin the fairytale.

I was pretty sure that I would never change my mind. Not one hundred percent sure, but pretty close. I kept telling myself that if I reached a certain age and still had no children, then I would be right here in this chair, getting cut and pasted as if I were being edited in Photoshop. When I reached that age, I still had no children. I had the freedom I wanted, though, and I roamed the globe with a woman who had that same sense of liberty and excitement. I expressed to her early on that I didn't want children. She said that she was okay with that but was honest that maybe after we had conquered the world, she might want children. She insisted she would respect my wish to not have them, but as the future neared, she discouraged me from cutting the cord.

I didn't want to upset her, so I didn't go through with it. One day she caught herself daydreaming out loud to me about our future children, and I bluntly said, "If you REALLY want to have kids, then you shouldn't be with the guy who REALLY doesn't want kids, and we should end this relationship now." I know I'd hurt her feelings. The tears were a dead giveaway. But even after that experience, I didn't muster up the courage to do what I really wanted to do. I knew having a vasectomy was her red line that I couldn't cross.

I didn't want to upset my parents either. While my parents were polite about my certainty that I wasn't interested in having kids, they silently prayed that the nice young lady I was with for five years would be the mother of their grandkids. My dad likes to say, "If a woman wants you to have kids, she will make you a father." For the longest time, he said that as if it were equally a statement of fact and a hope. That line was probably the last thing I thought about before I swiped my card to pay for what I called my "man-bortion."

My parents surely fantasized about spoiling their grandchildren with sugar highs and fancy gifts in ways they never did to their own children. With grandparents, it almost seems like payback for the time they were caught in that awkward and frustrating situation in Mickey D's where the kids insisted on two toys and wouldn't stop crying.

I sometimes see them in line, envision myself in those moments, and think, "What would I do as a parent here?" I always reach the same conclusion: adoption agency. Society generally frowns upon people who give up their kids for adoption. The shame around placing a child in a home where they could be better provided for is greater than keeping them in a home where their existence challenges a parent's sanity. I lack that kind of shame. I'd show up to Christmas dinner without Lil Dane ready to eat and open his gifts in his absence. I wouldn't care what people at dinner had to say. They can't pass judgment on me. They spend two hours a year with him.

That's more time than my brother Julian was allowed to spend with his daughter. All four of my brothers have children. Julian has one daughter from an ex-girlfriend in the UK, where he was born and raised. In 2012, he was embroiled in a bitter court battle just to be able to see his daughter. My brother was a great guy who at one time paid his ex-girlfriend the equivalent of $4000 a month. Still, she denied him the right to see his child. He spent close to $100,000 in legal costs to win his case. When the Scottish judge ruled in his favor, his daughter's mother moved from Scotland to Ipswich, England, where in order to enforce the order, he would have to start the process over.

He was heartbroken in 2015 when I hung out with him on vacation in Brazil. He decided to take a year off to travel the world, and we got together for a few days in Rio. Rio is one of the most exciting cities in the world. Still, heavy on my brother's heart was the fact that he hadn't seen his daughter in three years. And he never did again. The next time his daughter was allowed to see him was at his funeral in 2020. My brother died of a heart attack a month after his 50th birthday.

My friends with kids openly complained about their children, from their behavior to the cost of having kids to bad experiences with the other parent, so much so that I began a running joke where I'd say, "That's reason number 108 why I never had children." The number always changed, but it remained some astronomical figure to affirm that I had made the right choice. Still, despite some of the nastiest things they would say about parenthood and even about their children themselves, they eventually came back to saying, "I'm happy that I became a parent." Every time I hear that I can't help but think that if this is what happiness looks like, then I'm better off being depressed.

I knew what to expect from depression; I had battled it all my life. I knew it would come around, but I always knew what to expect. Unlike a child, it would eventually go back to wherever it came from. I know all the ugly things depression says to me. It had been saying those things to me since I was a child myself. It told me I wasn't strong enough and would never amount to anything. It told me that no one would find me attractive and that I could never earn enough to maintain a stable relationship. It told me a lot of things, including that it hated me.

My depression returned less often as I got older, but those messages heavily influenced the man I became. They shaped both my wildest behaviors and my low-risk tolerance. Depression made me happier knowing that I had not failed than I would've been knowing that I succeeded. And it taught me to always have an exit strategy.

Plan B could always be purchased at the drug store, whenever it's not sold out. But the power to take it lay in someone else's hands. I was still submitting to another person's will, that person who shared my same lustful desires just moments before, but may veer from my ideological desires. I have to ensure for myself that there is a plan C or a plan D or that no backup plan is needed. Men often claim the mantle of self-determination but wither like old unwanted Valentine's Day flowers with regards to the flesh. Plan C was always reactionary as opposed to proactive. Intimacy, love, lust, ego, and fear co-opt us into not taking action and what I fear most in life is action being taken against me.

For most of my adulthood, I viewed parenthood as a threat to the world of opportunities. The opportunity to travel, move to a foreign land, fly first class or on private jets and sail the oceans in the SS Dane Reid. These were distant dreams for the most part, but by age forty, I had actualized at least one of those dreams by stepping across 25 borders, although only by way of economy coach. Without the stress of providing for another person, I could at least provide my Instagram followers with the illusion that my life was complete.

What society thought I should have was travel, adventure, and a family, but my Bank of America account said, "Pick one," so I chose the one that mattered most to me; the one that I had always wanted ever since I was a child. I had always wanted to build a nest but didn't want to fill it with eggs. It's not that I have never experienced the fatherhood instinct, but my better judgment and future projections of self kept me from making purposeful errors. Even when I felt like I wanted a kid, I didn't want to be a parent. And in those rare moments when I wanted to be a parent, I didn't want a kid. I decided to slam the door for the sake of everyone who might be affected by my conflicting thoughts.

I recognize that I am also closing other doors of opportunity for prospective partners. Following my family's traditions, I have always wanted a wife. But veering away sharply from tradition, I wanted one who also shared in my vision for a life without children. This presented a challenge because of my other expectations and hopes for a wife. I want an educated woman who is loving and shares my love language. One who makes for great conversation and shares interests, communication styles, sense of humor, adventure for travel, and the same sense of boredom when we are at home together. I know the type of woman I'm physically attracted to and the type of woman I physically attract, and all of these things would have to meet at the junction of a child-free life to make it work.

What's the alternative to the burning flesh? Birth control? Adults have always encouraged teens to use condoms. But adults have always had a dirty secret that they kept from those teens. As I got older, I realized that people only used condoms with *new* partners. Few people used them with established partners. And when I say established, I mean someone they may have hooked up with three or more times. The psychology of it goes that the first two times, it was just for fun and a fun time isn't worth dying over or having a child over (Blackmon, 2022). But the third time is different. Nobody is gonna keep hooking up with someone they think has a deadly disease. This is the kind of logic that adults have engaged in since the invention of the rubber. The other dirty secret is that adults are just as reckless as teens.

In lieu of the condom, people often opt for the most viable birth control options, which usually means the woman pops the daily pill. Since their invention by Gregory Pincus and John Rock in the 1950s, birth control pills have become the number one go-to method for preventing pregnancy (Marsh & Ronner, 2008). The responsibility of preventing birth, much like the responsibility of raising children, has mostly fallen on women's ovaries. But the pill, like other forms of contraception like implants and injections, comes with its own set of risks. These risks to women's health have widely been deemed acceptable by drug developers, but at the time of this book, only a vasectomy has been shown to be an acceptable preventative method of pregnancy for men.

I take issue with that. Most of the women I have partnered with throughout my dating life have been on birth control at some point. It's advantageous to the guy who doesn't want children to encourage his woman to take them. But throughout the years, I realized that birth control pills don't just come with a list of acceptable reactions. They come with a list of *unacceptable* ones too. And when you actually love the person you are with, it's hard to ignore those risks.

I've dated women with a sexual appetite that rivaled that of the Hamburglar's glut for Big Macs, who, after starting on the birth control pill, shunned sex like Florida school boards shun books on diversity. My penis was all-out banned. I've had girlfriends whose entire demeanor changed after being on the pill. They started having wild mood swings, and we began arguing more frequently and intensely. That's not unusual. It was the birth control pill that led to the fights between Mr. and Mrs. Smith. That secret agent stuff was just a cover. She started taking birth control pills, and the next thing you know, she was trying to blow up her husband.

One of my ex-girlfriends, Brittany, developed severe acne from being on birth control pills. I've heard of women whose skin cleared up as a result of birth control pills too, but not so for Brittany. I felt bad for her because she was very self-conscious. We loved intimacy with one another, but only one of us had to make that sacrifice.

Apart from mood swings, acne, depressed sex drive, headaches, random vaginal bleeding, fatigue, breast tenderness, and nausea, some women must contend with another big issue: blood clots. I'm not talking about the angry machete-wielding dread you tried to avoid when you wandered off the resort in Montego Bay. No, I'm talking about actual, life-threatening internal blood clots (Martin et al., 2016). By the time I was 29, one of my ex-girlfriends, who was a year younger, suffered a stroke as a result of taking birth control pills. We had parted years prior, and she was dating someone else, but we remained friends. When I found out, I was torn in a way I had never been. If birth control could do this to someone I used to love, then it could do this to someone I presently love. But the answer at 29 was less apparent than it became at 40. At 29, I wasn't ready to be the one to prevent birth, arguments, acne, and strokes.

At 40, it became much clearer. Maybe those wise words from Smokey the Bear finally hit home: "Only you can prevent forest fires. Only you." I was finally having fun. But all that could go up in smoke with just one spark in the middle of the night. So I decided I'd rather let my vas deferens burn. This one's for you, Smokey. Here's what you tell them when they ask that burning question, "Why don't you want kids?"

Chapter 2
Reason # 137
There's Nothing a Kid Can't Break

Kids break things. I know. I used to break things. I broke a lot of things until my parents finally broke my buttocks in two. When you're a child, you don't know the value of things. You don't know anything about quality or style. Children don't associate the items in their homes with the man hours traded at work. Everything is worthless in a world of infinite wealth. Not that my parents were wealthy, but when you've been given everything from the moment the doctor first smacked you, you think there is nothing that can't be replaced. And for a lot of kids, that's the last smack they will ever receive, further incentivizing them to ravage and ransack everything in their path. It's like kids just want to see how much they can destroy and get away with.

Nowadays, there are entire businesses where adults pay to break things. Talk about putting your skills to work. I should've invented this. They call them rage rooms. But when I was a toddler, every room was a rage room, except it was my parents who had to pay. I hung from things, swung from things, smashed things, and trashed things. When my parents would ask if I was the one who broke things, I lied. It's not like we had security cameras in the house. How would they know it was me, except for the fact that every crime scene reeked of a 3-year-old's doing? Of course, my parents always knew, which resulted in double the punishments: one for breaking things and another for lying. My older brother always told on me anyway.

He was probably the one who snitched on me the day I went for a joy ride on the kitchen cabinet door. It was my first experience with swinging, and it was more fun than you could imagine. But who knew there was a weight limit for a cabinet door? You would think that they would warn a kid. I couldn't read back then, but they should've at least put a picture of a three-year-old swinging on it with a circle and a diagonal line going through it. I might have heeded the warning. But nooooooo! Due to the manufacturer's negligence, the door went flying off and I took flight with it. I injured my bum. The cabinet door hinge was a goner, and I was distraught. But instead of consoling me, my mother injured my bum yet again and then sent me crying and screaming to timeout. If I had been born just 10 years later this wouldn't have happened. My parents would've consoled me, patched up my injuries, and sued the cabinet makers. Darn timing.

Around the same time in my life, we had pet parakeets. I was always playing with the cage and would try to slide my little fingers through the grooves so that I could touch them. I didn't know how to open the cage at the time. The parakeets were so fascinating to me. Nobody else in our house could fly, so I always got a kick out of watching them spread their wings. Like all kids at that age, I was a shorty who chased the birds around the house whenever they were set free. I couldn't reach them. They were flying too high up, but occasionally they would land on something, and I figured that this was my chance to pet them. I wanted to play one day with our last parakeet. The others had died of natural causes. My mother let it out of the cage, and it took off flying throughout the house. It landed on top of an open door, many feet above my limited reach, and I remember encouraging it to come down and play with me. It didn't, but I was a rather smart cookie. I solved problems with ingenuity. So what would a determined, 3-year-old problem solver do in this situation? You guessed it. I slammed the door! I slammed it hard and fast too. Unfortunately, when our pet parakeet came down, he didn't feel like playing. He never felt like doing anything ever again. And what did my parents do about his permanent bout with depression? They blamed me, and I got another spanking. If the damn parakeet didn't want to play, all he had to do was say so. It's not like he couldn't talk.

No object in our house was safe. I once broke the glass layer on my mother's antique coffee table. My cousin Delia helped me with that one. I wanted to lift it up and slide something in between the glass and the table, and it was heavy, so I solicited her help. She was hesitant but eventually gave it a try. It was her job to hold the glass up while I slid paper or something under it. I thought she had a good grip, but obviously not. The glass came crashing down and broke into three pieces. Delia made a run for it. My mother heard the glass break and blamed me for it. Yes, it was my idea, but Delia was directly responsible for the breakage. Why did I have to get all the punishment? I was hauled off to toddler prison again. I spent more time "Up Against The Wall" than Redneck Mother. YouTube that song. You'll see what I mean.

I also used to break my mother's clothespins and attach paper wings to them to make them into little airplanes. This was New York City in the 1980's, when people used to hang their clothes outside to dry. It was annoying for my mother when I broke her pins in half to play with them, but that wasn't the major issue. The issue was that after these clothespin airliners took off, they needed a place to land. I liked landing mine in the electrical sockets. When my parents realized I was sticking objects in the sockets, they warned me not to and inserted those little removable plastic covers. I simply removed them and put them back when I finished landing my passengers safely. But one day, things didn't go so well. I was cleared for landing just like every other day, and out of nowhere, the plane was struck by lightning. I was shocked, literally and figuratively. But when I started crying, I wasn't consoled for almost being fried to death. No, it was back to time out. They didn't treat Captain Sully like that when his plane went down due to a bird strike. I both got electrocuted and struck a bird and didn't even make the news. But just like the airline that Sullenberger worked for, U.S. Airways, mine went out of business too that day. I didn't want to work there anymore anyway. The compensation sucked ass.

The terrible twos and threes come at a cost for parents. I remember riding in one of my friend's cars one day. I looked back at the empty car seat, frowning at the sheer chaos in the back seat. Her son wasn't in the car, but he definitely left his mark. The seat itself was marred as if a viscous tiger had gotten hold of it. Too bad he gnawed on the seat instead of eating the chicken nuggets stuck to the upholstery. Anything and everything that should not be in a car was back there. There was no cleaning it up. She would've had to replace the entire back row.

Now the mantle of "home desolation champion" has been passed down to my brother's daughters. They are the most beautiful and adorable nieces any uncle could ask for. If you argue with me about that I'll have to show you the pictures. You will lose. But they are also household terrors. I went to my brother's house in Jersey last year and he showed me all the things around the house the girls had torpedoed. I looked over at those gorgeous, innocent little faces and thought, "How could this be?" They don't look rambunctious. Every time I see them, they're sitting quietly in front of the TV, or patiently waiting while the grown-ups talk. Obviously, some other kids must be sneaking into his house and defacing the once white walls. My nieces were accused of swinging from the curtains and destroying them. Those curtains were annihilated. That's gotta be the work of some boys, not my innocent nieces. But to be on the safe side, I banned my nieces from visiting my home in Georgia. They are welcome to swing by when they turn 21. Until then, I'll leave the light on in the guestroom for my brother and sister-in-law in case they come to visit, but those badass kids have to stay at Motel 6. They can stay at Tom Walker's house, or even Tom Bodett's, but not mine.

When kids aren't breaking things, they are being messy. How many times do you have to tell a kid to pick up the toys off the floor? How many times do you as a parent nearly lose your life to a Lego block left on the stairs? Kids leave everything everywhere without consideration for safety or aesthetics. And over time, they wear the parents down to the point that the parents don't care anymore. Eventually, parents find chocolate pudding pops in the laundry basket and don't even flinch. Teens sleep on their beds with a mound of dirty clothing that makes their rooms smell like a dead animal is lodged in the walls, and the parents just concede defeat by closing the bedroom door. Now, not only does their son not have to wash and fold his clothes, but he also has complete autonomy to watch X-videos all evening until he falls asleep. But as long as he's happy, the parents don't let what he does in there rub them the wrong way.

Kids mess things up in the digital world too. They always want to borrow your devices. But when you get them back, things are never the same. Your icons are in different places. Your Netflix account is littered with suggestions for crap like Fuller House, Captain Underpants, and Transformers Rescue Bots. The only time this works to your advantage is when they get to be a teenager and use your computer, you can blame them for your questionable search history. But until then, you must suffer through trying to figure out WTF is "Avatar-The Last Airbender." At least they are only ruining your suggestions and not the computers. Oh wait, they do that too. You ever watch a child zipping through the computer and wonder, "How did they learn that so fast?" It's because they have no fear of clicking random buttons. Kids will click a red button on your laptop labeled "Virus" without consideration for the consequences. They only stop clicking when the laptop freezes and a pop-up demanding that you pay a hacker 1000 bitcoins appears on the screen. Defiant, you decide not to pay the ransom, until you realize that your son just messed up your work computer. Handing over your devices to your kids is like handing over your credit cards to Anna Delvey. They're just gonna look at you stupidly when you get upset for the damage they caused.

My life isn't child proofed. I don't want it to be child proofed. I want to decorate my house with style and not have to bolt my stair-step bookcase to the wall stud to keep some kid from flattening himself. I like vases on my coffee table and don't want them used for bowling pins. And I love art, but I don't need it drawn on the walls, nor do I think handprints on the stairwell wall are exactly Picasso-esque. Use the handrails for goodness' sake. The anxiety I experience every time someone brings their child over to my crib is akin to that of people living in Kansas during tornado season. Kids will tear the roof off your house if you let them. I couldn't imagine resigning myself to a storm lasting 216 months. No thanks. As for me and my house, we'll steer clear of tornado alley.

Chapter 3
Reason # 430
Because STFU

They were the cool kids. They met each other in a nightclub. She was the pretty girl who all the guys tried talking to. He was the smart, smooth, and well-dressed guy who watched all the guys strike out with her before he made his move. The club closed at 3 AM. He moved in on her at 2:15, bumping into her as he walked past her, intentionally spilling her drink on his fancy shirt. She made a big deal of it, apologizing profusely. He brushed it off, although casually informing her that she had ruined an Armani. Her guilt got him a few dances, her phone number, her hand in marriage, and four babies.

Ben and Jessica's first daughter Jennifer (aka Benji), was born, and things quickly changed. They tried to maintain their coolness but quickly realized that being full-time professionals, full-time parents, and a functional couple was not going to work. Something had to give. So coolness got cut, and functional couple would follow in years to come. Both parents worked early in the morning, but Jessica was the primary caretaker. Most nights when Benji cried, Jessica was the one to get up and feed her and rock her back to sleep, but sometimes it would take hours to get her to stop crying. Ben and Jessica were both becoming cranky and severely sleep-deprived.

One night Ben stopped his wife from getting up. "Don't worry, honey. You rest. I got this." Mom may have thought dad was giving her a well-deserved break, but he wasn't. It's these precious moments when a dad volunteers to get up to rock the baby back to sleep where his true instincts come out: like telling the kid to STFU. Mom would've rocked the baby forever before she stopped screaming. But dad had some special kind of magic touch, something he had learned from Cliff Huxtable: a shot of liquid Benadryl added to the formula. In fact, it worked so well that Ben continued lacing his daughter's beverages until she moved out to go to college. It got so bad that his wife had Benji tested for narcolepsy.

I called Ben one day. We liked to talk about big ideas. I had been thinking about how we could resolve the conflicts in the Middle East. It was a genius plan. No shots fired. All I needed was for Ben to listen, and the whole situation would've been over. By this time, his daughter was 3 years old. He picked up the phone. "Hey, Ben!" "What's up, Dane?" "I have a solution to the world's problems. All we gotta do is......" I was interrupted. "Whaaa!" It was the sound of Benji in the background crying her lungs out. "I'm sorry, Dane. Benji is having a meltdown today." Benji was having a meltdown the last time I spoke to Ben, too. In fact, Benji had daily meltdowns. This one was extra loud. I could hardly hear myself talking to him. "Hey Ben, have you tried the Shut the Fuck Up Method yet?" "I can't. She repeats everything. Then she'll go to daycare telling all the other kids to STFU, and we'll hear about it from her teachers. Plus, my wife will get angry with me." Poor Ben was stuck. So I, the unmarried guy, said, "Then just tell your wife to STFU, too." I had the solution to world peace, but I clearly knew nothing about promoting a peaceful marriage.

Ben and I got off the phone. A few weeks later, he called me from the car on his way home from work, like all married guys do, and told me that Benji came home telling him and his wife to STFU. Apparently, she learned it from another kid whose dad couldn't take the noise anymore. At least, that was the official account the substitute teacher gave. I was a sub for five years myself. I don't know if I'm buying that story.

The desire to tell a kid to STFU doesn't end when the kid is a toddler. It lasts their entire childhood. I love having adult conversations like the one I tried to have with Ben. Throughout my life, I have attempted these exchanges with parents only to be put on hold while they resolve some issue with their kids saying or doing something they shouldn't. A lot of it is simply interrupting conversations, which annoys the crap out of me. I couldn't imagine living my life where I am always instructing a little person to wait until I'm finished talking. How many times does a parent have to say, "When you see me talking to someone…?" It would exhaust me. Kids' certainty that their issue takes precedence over all others is in direct conflict with my patience and my belief that my issues take precedence over everyone else's.

We've all heard how kids also say the darndest things. Sure, they say some things that make you laugh, but other things they say make you want to tell them to STFU. Like when they snitch on you. Ben was always getting snitched on by his kids. They were like the CIA. Back in my day, if I ever shared any of my parents' business, I would've been reported as MIA. Ben couldn't hide anything. When he eventually had four daughters, their ears were listening everywhere he went. Once, we were talking while he was on the way home from work when he realized the youngest was still strapped into the car seat in the back. He had gone to work and forgotten to drop her off at the babysitter. After that, he had to stop calling me from the car. That night in bed, his wife said to him, "So, you wish you could fake your death and hide somewhere where you could indulge in hookers and blow, huh?" Ben was shocked. How the hell did his wife know all that? The baby was only 10 months old. Turns out that snitching on Ben were her first words.

Ben wasn't the only one who complained. Jessica had her own stress too. She spent the most time with the girls, and they were some combative little devils. The kids ruled the house, and when the parents dared to challenge their behavior, they were met with fierce backtalk. I tried backtalk once and still have a faint hand mark on my face from my mother. I was almost grown at the time but obviously not grown enough. At 17, I had finally mustered up the courage to give it a shot. The result was being hit harder than a Mark McGuire home run. Someone should've reported my mother to both child services and Major League Baseball for steroid use.

But these kids had no fear. Benji put her little sister in the dryer and was about to turn it on just before Jessica saw what was happening and stopped it. When Jessica tried admonishing Benji for her dangerous actions, Benji pointed at Jessica and yelled, "Don't you tell me what to do!" If this wasn't a STFU moment, I don't know what was. But Jessica, despite her instincts from being raised in the South Bronx, exhibited restraint. She had accepted what would've been unacceptable in my parents' house, from a little girl who still couldn't remember to wipe from front to back.

I had a slight taste of what Ben and Jessica experienced. When I was 19, I came back to New York for the summer from college. New York was home. I always loved coming back to the loads of diverse women walking, busing, and cycling around the city. I was staying with my family, and my closest cousin Sharon had her first daughter, Kiarah. We were just 19. What did we know about kids? I was in New York to practice making babies, not to actually make them. But Sharon had taken it a step further. Sharon and I grew up just blocks away from each other. We did a lot of the same stuff growing up and hung out a lot together. We always had a friendly and somewhat competitive relationship. But I was definitely not going to try and one-up her on this having babies stuff. No thanks. You win, Sharon.

I slept every night that summer in Sharon's room, on the floor next to the crib. In the daytime, I would pick up my sleeping bag and roam the city. But there were lots of days that I was a zombie. Kiarah was a newborn, and she cried at night like all babies. One night when Kiarah was wailing with her high-pitched cry, I woke up in a fog. All I could remember was Sharon's mother quickly coming into the room and turning the light on. I thought it was a fire emergency. I didn't know WTF was going on. My aunt stepped over me to reach the crib. "Oh no. Please, firelady, save me." You know those moments when you're just waking up and you're in a daze? This was that moment when I almost yelled at the firetruck's siren to "Shut The Fuck Up!" But I paused, wiped that crusty stuff from my eye, looked up, and realized that the house was not ablaze. It was Kiarah screaming for her nighttime bottle. Sharon and my aunt pulled out the hose, put out the fire, and rescued us all. After that, I moved my sleeping bag to the living room, where I slept for the rest of the summer.

I went back to New York every summer during college. I had a chance to see Kiarah grow each time, and at 2 years old, she was very inquisitive. Once I was driving Sharon and Kiarah somewhere when Kiarah asked me something about cars. I don't remember the exact question, but it was innocent, so I answered her. But her next question set off a chain of back-and-forth questions and responses that would inevitably end with me trying to explain string theory to a 2 -year old. After I answered the car question, she asked, "But Why?" I answered her, and she followed up with about ten more "whys." I needed some help here. (Sharon, can you control your daughter?) I even told her that I didn't know the answer to everything and she still kept asking "Why?" Was this kid trolling me? I was getting frustrated. I was getting STFU frustrated.

Sharon was frustrated too. She became annoyed with the exchange. This was like a UFC fight where one fighter is beating the hell out of the other and won't stop, and the ref hasn't intervened. I think she wanted to tell Kiarah to STFU, too, but I suspect that if Kiarah had asked "Why?" as a response, Sharon would've been carted off to Rikers.

Kiarah didn't know it, but that day, she changed my life. I realized that parents didn't just teach their children things; children teach their parents things too. I learned from Kiarah how to question things, to think deeper, and that just when I think I have the answer, always ask more questions. It's shaped what kind of thinker I am today. I had a chance to watch Kiarah mature from a baby who interrupted my sleep, to an annoying toddler, and now into a bold, intelligent woman who challenges the status quo. My only wish for her is that one day some smart-ass little kid gets in her car and annoys the hell out of her. Hopefully, she'll keep it cool and not tell the kid to STFU.

Chapter 4
Reason #45
But They Want to Travel Too

In the early 2000s, people traveled for business or pleasure, but not like what we see today. There weren't a million travel vloggers on YouTube exposing us to the world through the lens of their GoPros or smartphones. In fact, there were no GoPros, Apple hadn't unveiled the iPhone yet, and YouTube didn't come out until 2005. Plus, airline travel was expensive. If you wanted to see the world, you had to tune into the travel channel where you could drool over the lifestyles of the rich and famous but never touch the lifestyles of the average villager. You could see the champagne popping and boat hopping, but never would you see the hostel living and the local street food eating. And worst of all, you could never talk to the locals.

That all changed after September 11, 2001. A lot of airlines went out of business as a result of abysmal sales (Blunk et al., 2006). TWA? Gone! US Air? Gone! Delta was on the brink of disappearing, too, and eventually merged with Northwestern. As a result of several bankruptcies, airlines in the U.S. needed to bring passengers back to the friendly skies. Their strategy? To make the skies less friendly but a lot more affordable. And it worked.

Spirit Airlines and others popularized packing people in planes like SPAM into a can and removing all the perks of flying like legroom, snacks, free bags, and any trace of human dignity. For less money, passengers got nothing but a seat, a sweaty guy who drooled on them while sleeping, and a plane full of people who flew so infrequently that they hollered "Y'ALL TRYING TO KILL ME!" every time there was slight turbulence. The big airlines quickly started following in the footsteps of these bare-fare, low-cost airlines by offering passengers similar perk-less flights. Over the next decade, travel took off. People went to more places more frequently, but it still was nothing like when Millennials came of age in the mid-2010s.

As travel was just starting to grow post 9/11, I met Adam at a Toastmasters meeting in Buckhead, Atlanta. We were near the end of the meeting when he showed up late. Instantly he captured everyone's attention. At the conclusion of the meeting, everyone wanted to talk to him. This made me curious. I introduced myself and asked him why everyone found him so fascinating. Adam had just come back from six months of traveling through South America. He was a young guy, maybe just a few years older than me, but didn't appear much wealthier. So I asked him the question that I grew to hear too many times over a decade later, "How do you afford to travel so much?"

Adam explained his secret. He worked at a job he hated for six months, lived with his parents in the basement of their home, saved all his money, quit, and then traveled until he ran out of money. After every adventure, he came home to his parents' basement, worked another crappy job, saved up money, quit, and then traveled again. It was wash, rinse, and repeat, and it earned him the admiration of a room full of professionals who all had great stable jobs, kids in private schools, luxury cars, and big homes in the most exclusive part of town. Everyone in the room wanted to be him, including me. His Toastmaster speeches were so much more interesting than anyone else's. They were flush with unique and exciting travel stories, while the other speeches were just… bland. I wanted to be like Adam. He was Instagram before there was Instagram. He was what the Travel Channel lacked, a real traveler.

My younger brother and I had been planning a trip together since the early 2000s. I had always dreamt of traveling. It was going to be a man's trip. We had heard about a place in the Dominican Republic promising some of the most beautiful women in the Caribbean, and we were excited to see for ourselves. But life got in the way. By 2004, I got into an intense relationship with a woman I planned on marrying, and all bets were off. Then, in 2008, he got into an intense relationship with the love of his life and married her. Our relationships intersected, but once I broke things off with my fiancé in 2009, I didn't want to block the grid in his relationship. He and his wife were an incredible pair, but I was ready to have fun. I needed a travel buddy. Thank goodness I have a friend named Mike.

Mike was always down for an adventure. He had kids, but he wasn't always able to see them or be around them, so he was often available to be the world's greatest wingman. Mike used to drive from out of town to attend my birthday parties and stay at the club or restaurant partying longer than I would. He could drink way more than I could. Mike was the Mariano Rivera of nightlife. He came with extra benefits too. He knew how to talk to people, and he speaks multiple languages, including Spanish. He was perfect for my first international man's trip. We enlisted another friend Dillon, whom I knew from work. He was another guy who was always the life of the party. These men were the perfect operatives for what I had planned.

My wild overseas adventures started in 2011. Mike and I planned this crazy trip where we drove to Orlando from Atlanta, flew to Miami, and then onto Puerta Plata, Dominican Republic. That in and of itself was a crazy trip that involved me evading the police, hooking up with a girl in Miami that I met once in a club in Atlanta, and missing my flight back to Atlanta because of it and meeting Andre and his crew. Who's Andre, you ask? Andre was the guy who straightened my travel path and changed my life.

Andre was with his friends standing at the gate in Miami, ready to board. I heard him talking about what they were going to get into when they got to D.R., so I started up a conversation with him. He asked if I had ever been to D.R. before. I told him, "No." He smiled, and like an eagle to a worm, he took me under his wing. Andre was cool like the underside of a pillow. He had been to D.R. more times to pick up chicks than I had been to Winn Dixie to pick up chicken. Recognizing that we didn't know what to expect upon arrival, he broke down all the places we needed to go, all the things we needed to do, and everything to avoid. He exchanged info with us, and when we arrived in Puerta Plata, we even saw him on the ground a few times during our stay. We had a blast, Mike and I, largely due to

Andre's advice. We also had a blast because we were young, wild, and free.

That first big boy trip was a success beyond imagination, and I spoke with Andre later and thanked him for his guidance. During our convo, he told me that D.R. was just the tip of the iceberg. He and his crew travel all over the world multiple times each year. He casually asked, "Do you want to go to Thailand with us?" I excitedly answered, "Hell Yeah!" Nobody in my family had ever been to Thailand. Unless they had served in the military, no one in my family had ever been that far around the globe. Most of my friends didn't do stuff like that, either. They went to the Caribbean and maybe Europe but not to exotic places. Not to far-off lands. This was life-altering for me. Months after meeting a stranger in a Miami airport, I was traveling for thirty hours door to door to hang out in a club on Walking Street in Pattaya. Along my journey, I met retirees my parents' age who told me stories of their trips around the world and advised me on what to do when I got to Thailand, just as Andre had done when I met him. They were retired teachers, scientists, and other professionals who were either empty nesters or never had kids. These were people who loved their globetrotting lifestyle and they were having the times of their lives.

I couldn't help but think about my parents. When I told them that I was going to do this, they didn't totally get it. As I met these older travelers, I wished my parents, who were now free from the responsibility of raising my brothers and me, could see what I was about to see. Obviously, if I had been to Walking Street before, I would've realized that maybe it wasn't the best place for my parents to visit, but there were plenty of other places that would've been appropriate. (Walking Street is Disneyland for adults who have their private parts out ready for action. It's an overload for your senses and was a lot for even me to take in.) That notwithstanding, I had my mother and father in mind the entire time, just wishing they could have some kind of "Wow" experience in life like what I was having, like what those retirees on the plane had all the time.

There was a common theme among the travelers I met back in 2011. They were all free. They had jobs that either gave them lots of vacation time and great pay, or they were retired and had lots of time to roam wherever the wind took them. And most of all, they were *not* responsible for children. This kind of life excites my brain cells. This was a life I was determined to live.

From there, I went back to the Dominican Republic, then to Colombia, and then back to Thailand. I went to Panama for the first of several visits, then to Mexico and back to the Dominican Republic. I spent a week in Hawaii as well, visiting family members who worked there. My adventures began taking me to places I had learned about in elementary school and always wanted to see. In 2015 I went to China, Hong Kong and Macau, where I met up with my brother Julian. Julian and I went on to Brazil that same year and had a blast, meeting and connecting with other expat strangers. I had gone from being a guy who was in fact afraid of flying, to a guy who spent so much time on flights that the flight attendants asked me to help serve other passengers.

I became that obnoxious meme that says, "Catch flights not feelings." During that season of life, I missed flights, slept in airports, and traversed long distances by bullet trains. I made it to Cuba before Obama okay'd it and met a Costa Rican girl there who became my girlfriend and travel companion for the next few years. She was child-free, and had a passport with more stamps than the local post office. She showed me around Costa Rica, took me touring through Europe, and partied with my cousin and me for New Year's Eve in Sydney Harbor. We snorkeled the Great Barrier Reef, she taught me a lot of Spanish, and I was enjoying life and posting it all on Instagram. I never realized the impact it was having on people.

Whenever I was back in Atlanta and went out into the streets, I heard from my nine-to-five parent friends the same few comments or questions. They said things like, "I loved the pictures from Machu Picchu." "That looked like a lot of fun at Iguazu Falls." "When is your next trip?" But what did I hear most? "I wish I could do that." The truth is that I wish they could do that too. After my relationship ended with my Costa Rican ex-novia, I struggled to find more travel buddies. My friends all had home lives. They had tween and teen kids. They were parents, not travel partners. They were the soccer moms and dads who talked about their kids scoring the winning goal. I was the guy with no kids asking, "Hey, you wanna go to Jamaica on Friday?"

The answer was almost always no. The looks on their faces rivaled that of Eeyore, and I was the optimistically naive Winnie, not understanding why they couldn't tag along. It was unreasonable to think they could drop everything to travel with me on such short notice. Often, it was unreasonable to think that they could take time off from work and find a sitter who could watch their kids so that they could travel with me *anytime* this year, or ever. The guy who won't even buy living plants for his house couldn't relate to the friends who barely had time to stop by his oxygen-less house to hang out.

I live a different life. I live Adam's life now. I travel because if I stand still in a world that is continuously moving, I feel like I am falling behind. I love my friends and family, but stories about them raising kids and going to jobs they hate just don't excite me, not since I met Adam and I learned that I could carve out a life story that could dare to be different. People get excited when I walk into the room now. They want to know my stories. They want to know how I afford to go where I go. They want to know what's next. I simply tell them, "Jamaica on Friday," and laugh to myself.

Chapter 5
Reason # 617
Everybody's Got
a Friend Named Mike

Everybody's got a friend named Mike. If you don't have one, go get you one. Mike is my ace. He's the life of the party. We've been all around the world together. Mike helped me get my first job. He also convinced me not to have kids. Inadvertently.

From the time I met Mike in our first year in college, he had mapped out his whole life. He was going to work as much as possible, graduate college, and have all his children young so he could enjoy his life by the time he was in his early 40s. He joined the army reserve with the promise that they would pay for college and that he would retire with a pension at 38. Well, the army never paid for college, but that's an entirely different story.

But Mike wasn't only a hard-working guy; he was already a hard-partying guy. His vices were alcohol, late nights, and women. He loved the ladies, and that made him the perfect wingman for my adventures.

Mike came into college already with a son who was with the mother back in Boston. He was my first good friend who had a child. It seemed strange to me. At 18, I was a kid myself, and all this talk about responsibility and retiring and working was a total buzz kill. But apart from his wild side, Mike knew what he wanted out of life.

By twenty, he was in a relationship with his college sweetheart, and they had a son as well. Apparently, Mike really knew how to make sons. I remember the night his second child was born. Mike and I were heading to the club when we got word that his girlfriend was having contractions. We did what anyone would've done: we sprang into action, turned around, took his girlfriend to the hospital, and waited… until the doctor told us that it would be hours before she delivered. So we went to the club, and celebrated the pending birth of his son before we returned to the hospital with hours to spare.

We were both excited. I don't know why I was excited. I was thinking, "Two children? Man, he's making a big mistake." But He was there for every moment of the birth. His girlfriend later told me that he almost passed out, but he never admitted to that. Afterward, Mike led me to the hospital nursery, where he counted his son's fingers and toes and jokingly bragged about how large his son's penis was. He was basking in the moment of fatherhood, but the moment was short-lived. His relationship with his girlfriend soured, and when she graduated, she returned home to New York with their son.

Following his breakup, Mike was back on the scene. We both had broken up with our girlfriends around the same time. Mike was far more successful with women at the time than I was. He met women everywhere–at school, in the bars, in the street, at the grocery store, and even at his job. He was fearless. Sometimes I would see him whisper in the ear of a random woman at the club, and she would give him a huge glowing smile. The next thing I knew, they were simulating sex acts on the dance floor. Mike could bump, grind, spin, and drop it low with a woman, all without ever spilling a drop of his drink. Whenever I got a second of his time, I would ask, "What did you say to her?" He always smiled and answered, "I just asked her to dance."

All that bumping and grinding inside the club led to bumping and grinding outside of it too. But while Mike never spilled his alcohol on any of his dance partners, he sure did spill his baby batter in his sex partners. He had obviously not mastered the skill of pulling out, something I had been practicing since my first girlfriend in high school. But Mike had two things that I didn't, the art of persuasion and a job. Mike was done having kids and the gift that convinced women he was the right one, for the time being, was the same gift that convinced them that he was *not* the right one to be their child's father. And so he paid, and they terminated.

Mike was now not only the first guy that I knew who had two children, he was the first guy I knew with a subscription service to the abortion clinic. Every time he entered the clinic, they would yell out his name as if he were Norm from Cheers. Fine, I may be exaggerating a bit. In hindsight, it was just a few times, resulting in fewer trips to the abortion clinic than I would eventually provoke.

Mike also had a talent for attracting the wrong women. I guess when you meet so many, there are bound to be some really bad ones. One woman I will never forget was Keke. I doubt Mike will ever forget her either. Keke, scorned by the fact that Mike never took her seriously, tried to ruin Mike's life. This wasn't Drake's Keke. This was the Ghettos Keke.

Mike dealt with Keke in a situation-ship for a few months and at the advice of myself and everyone around him, finally let her go. She just didn't have any class. Keke, angered by that, decided to get even. She called and stalked for months, but Mike stopped answering her calls.

Mike worked in the hotel business. Early in my travels and even in my business, he would get me vouchers for hotel stays. He started working in that industry back when we were in college and worked his way up to management. He was a proud worker, always clocking into work on time wearing a suit and tie. That was his norm. But one day at work was anything but normal.

He clocked in and started his normal work when he noticed in the cameras that the police were on site. It wasn't unusual for the cops to be at the hotel because of occasional domestic disturbances or reports of prostitution. The officers walked into the office and asked to speak to the supervisor. Mike directed them to his supervisor who was in the other office. The police were in the office with his supervisor for just minutes when the supervisor called for Mike to join them. He hardly had a chance to put both feet in the room before the police slapped him in cuffs. Dressed as if he had been embezzling millions from someone's stock portfolio, he demanded to know what this was about. The police said, "You're wanted for child abandonment." What the fuck is child abandonment?

Mike had no idea what was going on. Wearing the same suit that he showed up for work in, he had his day in court following a night in jail. The judge admonished "men like him for not taking care of their children." Mike, still confused, told the judge that he has two children, both of whom he financially supports. Everyone seemed confused. The judge asked him, "Do you know Keke?" "Yes, your honor, but we don't have a child together. I haven't seen Keke in a very long time," Mike explained. "Keke filed paperwork with the court claiming that you have a child together." Going off of the possibility that Mike could be telling the truth, the judge ordered that he have a paternity test immediately before he proceeded with the charges and referred the case to family court. Mike was released, but not before the damage was done. He had been embarrassed, jailed, and after calling his job in order to report back to work, terminated. His supervisor explained that he wouldn't tolerate "drama" in the workplace.

Mike reached out to the source of the drama to clear all of this up. Keke began, "Since you didn't want to be with me…" then went on ranting about why she was doing this. He told her that the court had ordered a paternity test, and she told him that she would not cooperate.

Mike, being the guy that he is, started buying things for the baby. Things like formula, clothing, and toys. I think it was in part because he wondered if the child was actually his and also because he wanted to put on a good face for the court. Keke wasn't working and received support from the state. Stepping up would look good in front of the judge. It was four months before he got his day in family court. Four months of putting on a good face and doing what he thought was the right thing.

When Mike finally had his day in court, the judge was swift in ordering that Mike pay child support. Mike was prepared with receipts from all the months that he had been supporting the child. The judge looked at the receipts and said, "Sir, these receipts qualify as gifts, not child support." Those gifts, as the court called it, totaled thousands of dollars. Mike, upset but still composed, pleaded with the court to enforce the paternity test order. The family court judge, almost as if it were just a suggestion, told Keke that she needed to bring the child in for the test.

Over the course of months, Mike paid what he was ordered to pay in child support and back support. His follow-up day in court finally came. He updated the judge that he was paying the ordered support but also that Keke was paying the judge no mind about the required paternity test. The judge addressed the matter with Keke and set another date for several months later. Meanwhile, Mike kept writing those checks.

Keke must've been a paralegal in her past life. She knew the system. I don't know if she had any other children or had any other Mikes in court, but she sure knew how to stall the courts. At the next court hearing, she still hadn't brought her bundle of coins to be paternity tested. Mike protested, bringing the court's attention to the fact that Keke flagrantly ignored the judge's orders. Judges may be biased in all manner of cases, but few have tolerance for people flouting their orders. This time the judge warned her that if she didn't get the child swabbed for a paternity test by the next court date, she would go to jail. It was several months more until then, and Keke waited until just a week prior before she complied.

What a surprise! Mike had been paying out a small fortune for nearly a year for a child that had a nearly zero percent chance of being his. And his chances of getting his money back were about as high too. Upon presenting the results to the judge, Mike drew attention to the fact that the court failed him by allowing her to draw out this process for nearly a year. They failed by causing him to pay child support for a child he didn't think was his. The system had failed when they arrested him and caused him to lose his job. He asked the court to remedy the situation that they were complicit in. "Your honor, she should be ordered to pay all of my money back." The judge replied, "I'm sorry, Sir. We cannot do that. You will have to take her to civil court to recover your losses." Men all around the world heard about that ruling and formed the organization MGTOW.

The fact that this happened to Mike isn't even the craziest part. The craziest thing is that it happened to him more than once. Keke must've scribbled Mike's name on the back of a bathroom stall because Mike got hit with a similar scenario by a woman that he married. I was there the night that she proposed to Mike and he half-heartedly mumbled yes because she did it in public at a restaurant. I don't remember her being pregnant then, but it happened right before Mike was shipped off to Afghanistan.

Truthfully, I didn't even know that he had married her. He was sent off to training for a few months and then to his mission, where he was almost killed by an IED. During those months of training, they were legally married, and she got pregnant. It wasn't until Mike returned home a year and a half later that he met his daughter. When I met her, it was because I ran into his girlfriend-turned-wife in the mall pushing a stroller. She was the one who shocked me with the news that they were married with a child. I hadn't seen Mike in a long while. The daughter looked just like him. I joked with him when he returned that he must've been making love in the mirror. That little girl loved her dad. Well, at least the guy she thought was her dad.

As was the case for so many other soldiers who returned from war, Mike and his wife had marital issues when he came home. The wedge was so great that his wife moved out. Mike's mother, solely on a mother's instinct, kept telling Mike that his daughter wasn't his daughter at all. So when Mike had custody of his daughter for several weeks, he took the three-year-old for DNA testing. The baby wasn't his. He filed for a divorce where in court he presented the evidence to the judge. His wife denied it before being confronted with the DNA test results. The judge, disgusted by Mrs. Mike, annulled their nuptials on the grounds of marriage fraud. His wife, according to the judge, rushed to marry Mike in hopes that if something happened to him in Afghanistan, she and her child would collect military benefits.

Mike has now started over at the very point he had planned on it all ending. He remarried and has a new child, a boy. His son is the love of his life. He's moved overseas, where he is a lot less stressed, and says he loves the opportunity to be a full-time dad and husband. I recently spoke to him on video chat, and he truly seems happy just being a family man. I sometimes think about all that went wrong in his journey to reach this point in life. He says he doesn't.

Chapter 6
Reason #122
I Don't Want the Responsibility

I had one job and one job only. My job was to clean the tank. Actually, my one job was to keep the fish alive. When I was a kid, I couldn't have a dog. Every kid wants a dog except for the few weirdo kids who want a cat. But my parents weren't keen on getting dog hair on their furniture, clothes, carpet, bed, etc. And they weren't gonna walk a dog either. And you know what? They knew I was too lazy to do it too.

So, after begging for years for a pet, I got... goldfish. A fish was a low-maintenance pet. I didn't have to walk it, pooper scoop it, pay it any mind, listen to it bark, bathe it, worry about it scratching or destroying anything. I know, at this point, you're probably calling me a heartless dog hater. But I promise you, I'm not heartless. I just don't like inconveniences. And bad smells. Anyway, back to the fish.

Anyone who has owned fish knows that cleaning the tank is the hardest part about owning them. You gotta take the fish out and put them in temporary housing, an Airbnb for fish of sorts. Then you have to scoop out the water little by little until there is nearly nothing left. Next, you take the rocks out and wash those because the rocks hide fish shit.

Well, I started off like gangbusters. I was feeding the fish and watching them swim around all the time. It was better than TV. But just like with other things, my interest quickly waned. I went back to watching TV because these fish stopped swimming like they used to. When I first got them, they used to do tricks. After a while, they didn't seem to care if I was entertained. I'd come up to the tank, and as if to remind me that it needed to be cleaned, they would shit in front of me. After about a month, the most interesting thing about them were the shit shows. That and when that white stuff started growing on them and their backs started arching. Who knew that was a sign that they were on their last fin? It would be lights out as soon as the lights went out. My boredom and neglect led to their demise as the tank got cloudier than Rudy Giuliani's judgment after a few drinks.

After the last one died, it was back to the Cosby Show. My parents were right. They knew that I wasn't gonna take care of fish, much less a dog. They knew that feeding and caring for a dog would have resulted in the same fate. All they had to do was look at how I never hung my clothes up in the closet to figure out that I never wanted to do extra work, even when it involved things I cared about. Hindsight should've been 20:20 on allowing me to watch Bill Cosby's rapey ass on TV. Maybe they figured I was too lazy to seek out some Spanish fly too, so I'd be okay.

I can't say much has changed. As an adult, I call myself a minimalist, but that's just code for "I don't own much, so I don't have to take care of much." I still don't have a dog. I still think cats are pets for crazy old ladies who live alone and have lost their sense of smell. I don't even own a real houseplant. Who's gonna water it when I'm off globetrotting? Or just sitting in my living room, not giving a fuck? Instead, I have fake plants courtesy of Ikea. They have some great planters there, too, by the way.

Now, can you imagine the same guy being responsible for another human being? A baby cries and relies on that guy to bring him/her their bottle. I picture myself yelling from the other room, "Cut the noise, kid, and get your own bottle." Or, how about having to get the kid off to elementary school? I picture myself yelling from the other room, "Wake up. Get Dressed! And hurry to school. You're late!" My dad used to do that, and I was late every day. I can't picture figuring out childcare, feeding the kid, taking them to the doctor, or to soccer practice. Imagine me having to work overtime or even an extra job to make ends meet all for the sake of a child. I have a liberal arts degree. I can hardly find one job, much less two.

When you sign up for parenthood, there are a lot more moving parts. There is a lot more to be responsible for. Not only are you signing up for the parenthood part, you're signing up for all of the things that *support* parenthood. You're signing up for school and long nights doing homework, even after you've finished a long day at work. You're signing up for parent/teacher conferences, and if you're anything like my parents, you might even become the PTA president. You have to keep the lights on. You have to feed the kids healthy food so they can stay focused in school. You have to provide a good example for them. That means I'd have to stop cussing and speak proper English. And that's just the tip of the iceberg, although I recognize that in practice, many parents don't care about some or any of them. But I grew up in a house with parents who did, so that was my idea of parenthood, and it still is.

I never understood responsibility. I never understood why people would add more complexity to their lives. I like things to be simple. I'm the guy who eats the same breakfast every day. It's just easier that way. Some people need variety. That means more work. I'm not that guy. Responsibility just seems a lot harder and a lot less enjoyable. So why do it? The best answer I have been able to get out of people is that it's the grown-up thing to do. But inventing someone else without good reason doesn't seem like the smart thing to do. It feels as if it's being done just because you're "supposed to."

We need people to step up. As long as there are people left on the planet, someone has to join the armed forces and do that submarine duty. Someone has to run into that fire to rescue that family. Somebody has to clean up the mess that Trump left in his wake. We need inventors, investors, and money managers. We need nurse techs and Big Brothers and Big Sisters. We need people who will take on the high-paying jobs and the no-paying thankless ones too. If not, we can't function as a society.

I get it. Not all of us can have the luxury of living rent-free in our mother's basement. Society progresses not by doing the easy things, but by doing the hard things. At one time in history, humans were hunter/gatherers, and each member of the tribe was responsible for the rest of the tribe. We each had responsibilities. There was no CVS at the corner, so if you wanted to engage in your favorite activity, you could very likely end up being a parent. And someone had to go kill an ox or an ass while someone else watched the kids. When farming took off, those kids became necessary to help till the land and harvest the fruit. For the survival of the species, we all needed one another. But that's not who we are anymore. We have choices. We have CVS. We have other favorite activities. And we don't have to voluntarily make things harder. Kids make things harder. I'd rather have a V8. Or a cat.

Chapter 7
Reason #223
The Book of Brittany, Part 1

"I know this girl you would like. You two would get along well. You both love sex." That was all I needed to hear from my beloved cousin, who wanted to introduce me to her best friend. I was 23 and trying to find my way after breaking up with a girl I was sure was going to be my wife. In hindsight, with all my relationships that lasted more than a month, I had envisioned the woman being my wife. But that relationship lasted three years, which seemed like infinity at the time. In between, I dated other women, but I knew we weren't matches. No one offered me the level of excitement and sexual energy that my ex did.

At twenty-three, attraction and sexual energy were everything. We needed to get along with one another while standing up too, but how much we drove each other mad lying down was the true measure of "love." I had that kind of explosive love with two other women in my life, but what I was about to experience with Brittany was an entirely different thing.

I thought I had done it all and seen it all. My previous relationship was fiery. It was hyper-exploratory. No toe, earhole, or eye socket went unpoked. And it was always poked naturally. Back then, condoms were what later became of masks during the pandemic. Nobody wanted to wear them. In the name of freedom, we took our chances, and we neither got Covid nor pregnant from it. After a while, I began thinking, "What Boogie-Man?" I believed pregnancy was something that happened to other couples.

Over time, I started thinking the "Pulling Out Method" was 100% effective. A quick Google search would've told me it has a near 25% fail rate, but you couldn't tell me that based on my success. I had gotten so good at it that I started calling myself "Quick Withdraw McGraw" and touted my ability to roll off jokingly with friends. Sadly, despite the cleverness of the name, it never quite caught on.

So here I was, about to meet a hook-up that I had no idea would turn into a turbulent four-and-a-half-year relationship and the mother of three of my children. (I know what you're thinking. Just keep reading until the end. It'll all make sense eventually.) A person who would myth-bust all my delusions about rolling off just in time. A woman who would satisfy my body and anger my mind all to the same degree. A woman with whom I would form a destructive codependency, both of us overmedicating in indulgence to hide our pains and insecurities. We hit it off in all the wrong ways.

My cousin brought Brittany to meet me one afternoon. I came to the door, looked her up and down, grabbed her by the hand, and led her to the living room. She was tasty looking and timid all at the same time. She stood there, knowing exactly why she was being introduced to me. This was a hookup, and we were only getting to know each other for that reason. Still, she was my cousin's friend. I treated her as I would any woman I was considering to be a girlfriend. Respectfully. That day, we didn't hook up. We just talked for a while and decided on a time and date when we would see each other again. It wouldn't be long.

It was just two days later. I took the hour-long drive out to the university, where she went to school to pick her up and bring her back into the city. We didn't go straight to the bed. No, in fact, I took her to the zoo. She seemed super cool and laid back, and I enjoyed our previous conversations on the phone so much that I wanted to enjoy getting to know her in person. We discovered that we both had a love for Jeopardy. (Over the years, she destroyed me repeatedly while playing over the phone.)

We sat near the park talking and she expressed to me that guys never treated her well. They never wanted to know anything about her. I did. It was rare. Still, we both knew that I also wanted to know more about her abilities, and she expressed her curiosity about mine. She kissed me and asked to go back to my place. So we did, and we did it, and we did it again and again and again for the next several years.

I dropped her off that afternoon in front of her dorm. I kissed her, and she climbed out of my car to walk the 100-foot distance along the walkway to the dorm. I waited for her to reach the building entrance. Concerned, Brittany walked back to my car and asked if something was wrong. I said, "No. I'm just making sure you get into the building safely." Unaccustomed to any form of chivalry, she replied, "You don't have to do that. Nobody else ever has." She again gave me a strange look as she closed my door and walked to the dorm. All the way, she tracked to see if I had left. I hadn't. Not until she securely entered her dorm. Her past experience wasn't going to change my present behavior.

Brittany and I continued to get to know each other with more dates, mostly in the daytime. More restaurants. More movie matinees. More Jeopardy over the phone. And more incredible sex. It had been weeks of knowing each other and exploring each other's bodies when I felt something different. In a steamy session, she brought me to climax in the eruptive manner that I had only experienced with her. And at that moment, I had a divine feeling like never before. I remember it clearly. I had rolled off just as I had mastered over the years, but I had a strong sense that this time it didn't matter. "No. I'm being paranoid. I'm just coming to my post-sex senses where I'm able to think clearly and question what the hell am I doing."

Our relationship continued to grow in the next three months. We were happy. I was happy. We got along great. We never argued. We spoke daily and saw each other several times a week. She even started sneaking me into the dorms overnight. Her roommate was super cool and had other places to hang out. And when the semester ended, we found creative ways to see each other. Brittany returned home to the suburbs, where she lived with a strict religious father. He was a proud Muslim man, although the rest of the family didn't share his faith. Still, he ruled his house with an iron fist. Brittany, accompanied by her mother and younger sister, found her escape by attending church on Wednesdays and Sundays, where her father dared not enter.

Many of those times after she had driven to church with her mother and sister, I would show up and whisk her off to somewhere more interesting or intimate and return her to church in time to head home. It wasn't all the time. She really did enjoy church, but she often wanted to trade her sainthood for sins. I was happy to oblige. Her mother knew the game. Brittany was an adult capable of doing as she pleased, just not when her father was around.

Over these short few months, I spoke to my cousin a lot less. She hadn't calculated that Brittany and I would last months and decided to take a hands-off approach to our relationship. Somewhere in June, right when the summer began, my cousin seemed to disappear. I began to wonder whether she was happy for us or not. Whether she thought that she had made a mistake. Or if her best friend and cousin had traded her in for one another. So I called her.

It was August, just before the new school semester. I was happier than I had been in a long while. I had a partner. Things were great. Brittany and I had a great summer. But I found out in that conversation with my cousin that Brittany's summer was slightly more action-packed than mine. Hesitantly, my cousin advised me, "You need to talk to her. She's been hiding a few things from you. I don't want to be involved in y'all's relationship."

I couldn't imagine what she was hinting at. I pressed my cousin to tell me what was going on. I could hear in her voice that she didn't want to betray her friend's confidence but also couldn't betray her cousin. Finally, she spilled the beans. "You need to confront her about the guy in the church. The one who plays the drums. She started having sex with him in July." At that point, all the air was sucked out of the room. I was deflated. How could this happen? "Dane, please call her and talk to her. She's been hiding other things, but I will let her tell you."

So many emotions went through me. It was the first time I had ever been mad at her, and this one was a doozy. But I didn't hesitate. I called her. I was cool about it on the outside, but I was boiling inside. I wanted to hear her side of the story. "What happened? Why would you do this?" I asked. She felt cornered though, and like a New York City rat trying to defend a slice of pizza, she lashed out. "WHAT THE FUCK ARE YOU QUESTIONING ME FOR? THIS WAS ALWAYS NOTHING BUT A HOOKUP. YOU DIDN'T THINK THIS WAS SERIOUS? DID YOU? YOU WERE OUT FOR YOUR OWN, AND SO WAS I…" She went on and on. Her profanity-laden tirade continued against the man who had begun loving her.

We argued, and when the conversation was nearly over, I said, "My cousin told me there was something else you didn't tell me. What is it?" She nastily replied, "Since your cousin is telling you everything, then why don't you ask her? Since y'all are so close, you can go fuck her too." From there, it was all a blur. I couldn't talk to this slut anymore.

I followed up with my cousin shortly after my argument with Brittany. I couldn't believe that I invested in our relationship, only to be crapped on just as men had crapped on her before me. I described to my cousin how the conversation transpired, and she didn't seem surprised. She apologized for introducing us. But it wasn't her fault.

Ultimately I enjoyed my short time up until then and knew that, like a big boy, I would have to dust myself off and move on. "So did she tell you the rest?" my cousin inquired.

"No, what rest?" "Dane, back in June, she had a miscarriage. She was pregnant with your baby."

Stunned, I reflected on that intimate moment when a divine voice whispered in my ear. I knew it was true. Dusting myself off and moving on like a big boy just got a lot harder.

Chapter 8
Reason # 828
There's Never a Good Time to Have Kids

Brandy told me when I was twenty that there is never a good time in life to have kids. We were the same age, and she had already had one child and was considering number two. I thought that was a crappy idea, but she explained that for her, this was the ideal time to have her second baby with her boyfriend. Brandy and I worked together. It was my very first job. My goal was to work this call center position long enough to earn money for a down payment on my very first car, a Chevy. But Brandy thought bigger, belly bump bigger. She didn't want to have children too far apart, and if my memory serves me correctly, her first son was already two. She was working to take care of herself and him with the help of her son's father and her family. That was quite different from how I thought about life. I just wanted mobility so I could meet more girls and get back and forth to school without the MARTA (Atlanta's Rapid Transit System).

Brandy and Mike were similar. They had long-term goals. Mike worked alongside us at the same call center and was the one who helped me get the job. Brandy was a hot little thing. She was eye candy that I wanted to lick with my tongue, and I'm sure most men who saw her thought the same thing. It made me wonder why she would limit her young life by having another child. I asked her, and she responded, "Dane, if you wait for a convenient time in life to have children, you'll never have kids." Translated into "Dane-Latin" that meant "Dane, DON'T have kids. Period." That's not what she meant to say, but that's what I heard. She went on to explain the same kind of parent logic that Mike had. She already had one child and thought that completing her family branch early in life would free her up in her 40s while she was still young enough to hit up the club with her 21-year-old son and sing along with him to the latest rap tunes. I know a guy who did that. In the process, he got lucky, scored his son's girlfriend, married her, and they had three kids. If you cross your fingers and say Beetlejuice three times, this could be you too.

There are pros and cons to having children at a young age. When you're young, it's harder. You're essentially fighting an uphill battle. For some people, that's the fuel they need, but for many, that's the North Atlantic iceberg that sinks their ship. Millennials are the most educated and most traveled generation ever, but they are also burdened with the most student loans and biggest housing shortage (Morrison-Williams, 2022). Millennials began graduating college and entering the job market right when the 2008 financial crisis hit, so they weren't exactly off to a Boomer-esque start (Wolff-Mann, 2020).

On top of that, while their parents enjoyed a high quality of life during retirement from pensions, Millennials had to save their own coins in 401k's with hopes that their employers would do some kind of matching (Burchel, 2017). What made things worse was that no longer could workers expect to retire from the same job they started fresh out of college. To get pay raises and promotions, employees had, and still have to play the game of employment checkers, jumping from position to position and job to job just to get ahead.

I once got a job because I didn't have kids. It was a crappy, sub-ten dollar an hour job, but it was one I needed at the time. So did the mother who *didn't* get the job. I showed up at the interview, where I was one of several candidates. I was early because I lived less than a mile from the building. The interviewer asked me several questions pertaining to my qualifications but also some personal questions. I answered them. "Yes, I live close by." "No, I don't have any children." "Yes, I have reliable transportation." I didn't think anything of the questions. I figured he was just getting to know what kind of person I was. The interview went well, and he offered me the job on sight. I was surprised. He told me that there was another very qualified candidate who he was also very impressed with, but he picked me because I "lived closer than she did." This seemed to make sense to me, but when he leaned over toward me, he admitted something more sinister and discriminatory. He said, "I'm hiring you because the other candidate has two children, and mothers take too much time off when their kids get sick or when they have other parenting duties that prevent them from coming to work." Even then, I knew something was wrong with that. I probably didn't need that job as much as she did, but I took it anyway. The funny thing about that story is that that same guy fired me on the first day for being late. I guess he calculated that all wrong.

He's not the only one who thinks that way. American society isn't made for being a parent, so navigating it while having a child is extremely difficult (Miller, 2019). Employers all over the country factor in family when hiring mothers in particular (Aloi, 2005). I even spoke to a friend who admitted that she prefers to hire women with no children. The irony is that she herself has children, but she said that "when running a business, you have to have people you can always depend on, and it's hard to depend on mothers." That means selecting candidates who either haven't had children or candidates who have grown children. This complicates an already difficult career path for young parents.

It's tougher when you aren't where you want to be in life. For most parents, the dream is to create a comfortable life where their children end up better off than they were. Making your life better makes the lives of your children better by clearing a path for them to follow, or by giving them the freedom to create a better path. But when saddled with student debt, it's hard to reach that comfort point. Climbing the corporate ladder or trekking along the career trail are both long routes. For many people, it might not be until they are 40 years old before they reach a place where they can emotionally and financially support a child in a way that is fair to the child, plus be able to dedicate an ample amount of time to them (Villines, 2020). They say money is the root of all evil. Well, if that's true, then good child care, great school systems, health care, and quality time with your children are all the devil. Money is a *necessary* evil for raising kids, and establishing a strong financial footing makes things easier.

When you're a young parent, you grow with your children. As you are figuring things out and maturing, so is your little one. Can't sort out why your kid calls you by your first name and calls grandma "Mama?" It's probably because you resemble the kids in their class. Wanna know why they won't stop saying the "F word?" Look no further than your Spotify playlist. "Mama" doesn't play those kinds of songs. She's tuned into the Joel Osteen Radio Network, for which she pays 89.99 a month. Your only hope is that your kid doesn't combine the two and start telling the other kids, "Give me your F'ing lunch money or I swear to God somebody's getting hurt." That's how Kanye got his start. Donda was just 27 when Kanye was born. Those mixed messages made him into the man he is today. Is that the man you want your son to be? Seriously though, as you are trying to find yourself and still making the mistakes we all make when we are young, you are also responsible for making sure your children don't pick up on the errors you're still committing. A lot of people wonder, "Where did my child learn that?" In the words of the old Anti-Drug PSAs, "You alright! They Learned it By Watching You." Children pick up on things, recall them and act them out even when they've only witnessed you doing it once.

I wasn't sure about myself until I was 40. That was the same age I realized that a vasectomy was right for me. I had traveled the world, had crazy adventures, became comfortable with my money, and confident with my interactions with other people. I think that's the case with a lot of people. It's the point in life where you can say, "Yeah, I've done that already," and feel content if you never get to do it again. It's a reflection point where self-awareness and introspection can leave you unbothered by what other people say about you. At least, that's what happened to me. When I turned 40, the like and dislike button became the same. Neither was capable of defining me.

There are two trains of thought when it comes to deciding when to have kids. The first being the route that Brandy and Mike took. The second is to have your kids older, closer to 40 than 20, when you have had time to sort your life out, get to know yourself, and run wild and do stupid shit like nearly getting arrested for having sex with a stranger on a hotel balcony. I don't know where that last example came from. Honestly, I don't. But it seems like something that only people without kids should attempt.

If you're a woman, the time is ticking until your eggs dry up. And if you're a guy, you run a higher risk of your kids being autistic. Don't get mad at me, guys. Go to Home Depot, buy up all the tiki torches you can find, and march on down to your local epidemiologist's house and protest, because they're the ones who collect data on your old ass sperm. I'm just the messenger. A 2017 report in the Washington Post cites various studies conducted in Israel, California, Denmark, and Sweden showing men in their 40s were six times more likely to have autistic children than men in their 20s *(DeWeerdt, 2017)*. This doesn't mean you guys in West Virginia are exempt. They didn't mention this in the article, but having kids with your cousins increases those chances exponentially (Sandin et al., 2014).

Despite the risks, there are some advantages to having children when you are older. Obviously you are more likely to be established financially and emotionally *(Villines, 2020)*. Working with children for five years, anecdotally, I observed that children with older parents seemed much more mature, better behaved, and more focused on tasks. They avoided problems and better-resolved conflicts with other students. But the kids with parents who were younger were rowdier, more likely to have conflicts, less focused, and overall had poorer results. I observed the same results in many children who didn't have fathers in their lives. Of course, this was all just my perception working in one population of elementary-aged kids, but it was evident enough for me to form an opinion even then.

Older parents have more to teach their children. I'm reminded of a Jay-Z line that I repeat in my head all the time. He said, "Hov did that, so hopefully, you wouldn't have to go through that" *(Songfacts, n.d.)*. He goes on to tell his stories of growing up poor and hustling his way to the top. He had lived experience that through rap music, he was able to tell his stories, not to glorify his mistakes, but to warn others not to commit the same ones. Older parents are like Hov. They can tell their children from first-hand experience that putting that hand in the fire burns. It's different for younger parents who might be learning how to put the stove on for the first time. Young parents are still writing their stories, while older parents recollect theirs.

Older parents are more likely to own a home than younger parents. Older parents are more likely to consider things like school systems when deciding where to live. They are more likely to be involved in P.T.A., producing better results for their students (Ferrara, 2009).

Parent involvement can play a key role in children's success. None of this is to say that younger parents don't do some of the same things, but it's less likely.

But there are some disadvantages to being an older parent. I remember someone once asking me why I didn't have children. Whenever someone asked me that question, I had to consider who that person was before I reached down into my bag of answers. The person who asked was an older parent, so I answered by saying, "I'm 40 years old. I don't want to be 50 having to throw the ball around with a 10-year-old." They agreed. By the time their daughter turns 10, they're gonna need to press the fall alert device for assistance every time they want to get off the floor from playing Barbie. That excuse resonated with them. They knew it would be harder to participate in activities and relate to their kids on the same level that younger parents would. It would be harder to know the latest songs, trends in music and pop culture and know what their children were involved in online. They were less likely to get why their kids wanted their hair a certain way or used seemingly senseless terminology. Older people thought when something was "Lit" you needed to call the fire department and that if your clothes had "drip," you needed to go dry off.

Older parents are also likely to hang onto old values *(Villines, 2020)*. Some of those values can be good. My grandmother used to say that anytime someone came to your house, you should offer them something to eat if you have something and if you don't, at least offer a glass of water. She learned that when she was younger. I'm selfish, so I only offer people a bottle of water. Plus, I'm the unmarried dude. The food in my fridge has to stretch the entire week. Still, that value stuck with me from her teachings. Another downside is that older people are often steeped in prejudice toward people and situations in an ever-changing world. They have a difficult time keeping up with and respecting those changes. They even fight change because it's hard for them to adapt, so they risk being left behind while their children try to explain why everyone else is surfing with the tide.

In my short life, I have seen lots of changes that Boomers would've never predicted and many still don't want. I've witnessed a black president being elected twice, gay marriage becoming the law of the land, biracial dating becoming the norm, and widespread adoption of tattoos. If you're a Millennial or Gen-Z, you take all of that for granted. But when I was a kid, there was just one dude who was tatted from head to toe standing on the boardwalk at Coney Island, and you had to pay to take pictures with him using your disposable camera. That all changed as tattoos and smartphone cameras became ubiquitous, and that guy's schtick faded into nothing special. I just hope he didn't kill himself in front of city hall after competition forced him out of work. That would be uber sad.

I feel bad for the parents who have one kid when they are young and turn around and have another when they're older. Those parents' lives are ruined from start to finish. Just when you think you only have a few more years to serve on this 18-year sentence, they find that body you buried at the bottom of the river, and you catch another 18-year charge. If only you hadn't killed it that infamous night, you wouldn't be restarting the clock. While you're helping your kid look for a good college to attend, they'll be helping you search through brochures for a nice retirement community for yourself.

One subset of people I've encountered who are hitting the reset button later in life is fathers. I am hearing more often than expected about dads who are having children at a later age for the second or even third time. These are fathers like my friend Mike who, for various reasons, didn't raise their children the first time around. People often underestimate the love that a father has for his children and villainize fathers for not being there for their kids when often those fathers were focused on providing for them, or were prevented from seeing them by their mothers (Crowley, 2008). These fathers seek redemption by starting new families, and attempting to do this time around what they couldn't the first time around. They love being dads.

I guess I'm more of a "leave the past in the past" type of guy. I loved my first Chevy, but I'll never buy another one. It was great back in 2004, but I drive something better now. I'm not interested in correcting the past. I thought deeply for years after that conversation with Brandy and I realized that the decision I made to run out the clock was the correct decision. I waited so long to decide that not making a decision became the decision. Certainly prior to my vasectomy, I had the option to have a child at any time. I know men who are in their 60s who have children. That's not my cup of tea. Plus, like I added before, I don't want my kid born with two heads. I'll be too old to figure out which one of them to throw the baseball toward.

Chapter 9
Reason #308
I'm Selfish and That's Okay

When I grew up in the '80s in New York, people used to walk down the street with boom boxes playing their music. Even as a four-year-old, I recognized the cool factor that brought attention their way as they strolled the block. Long before Radio Raheem got choked out by the cops, everyone thought playing their music loud enough for the whole community was the right thing to do. My older brothers had boom boxes. Back in those days, we played a lot of music in the house. But I didn't have one of my own, and I wanted to listen to the latest Michael Jackson, Phil Collins, New Edition and UTFO joints too. But I dared not touch my brother's boom boxes.

As Christmas was rolling around that year, I prayed to Jesus and Santa Claus that I would get my own portable boombox. Having two much older brothers, I didn't believe in Santa, but I certainly played up his existence that year. Christmas day was a "thank you Jesus" moment in musical history. I got my boombox. It was great. It had a station tuner, so I could listen to 98.7 KISS. It had a tape recorder

so I could record music from the radio and listen back later. It had...
Well, that's really all it had, but that's all a 4-year-old needed. And
best of all, it was all mine.

From as long as I could remember, my parents instilled in us
the adage, "God bless the child that's got his own." We shared the
same room, but we all had our own stuff in the house. We had our
own chairs at the kitchen table, our own forks and knives, and our
own cups. Later in life, we even had our own arrest records. It was
important to our parents that we had our own for many reasons. For
one, it taught us responsibility. We took pride in our own things, and
if we lost or broke something, it was all on us. Nobody was going to
loan you theirs. Plus, with three boys, having each of our own things
minimized conflicts. And lastly, I think my dad was reflecting on his
own childhood and wanted us to be better.

He often told us this totally believable story of growing up in
a house with eight brothers and sisters where they had to share
everything. He said that between the nine of them, they only had
one pair of shoes, so every morning, he would walk the eight miles
up a steep hill to school in the shoes and then walk back home to
hand them off to his younger brother. Then he would walk back to
school barefoot, and his younger brother would repeat his process
until the last child got to wear the shoes to school. My dad told us
that story countless times, I may add, to illustrate to us how hard he
had it growing up in comparison to how easy we had it, and to show
us how he had to share everything. But I don't know if I bought it.
My dad was the third child in his household, and his oldest sibling

was a girl. My dad doesn't seem like a guy who would wear his sister's shoes, so I'm gonna call BS here. Still, I do know that he had to unwillingly share a lot of other things. His experiences as a child shaped the way he raised us and made me the proud, selfish man I am today.

While my dad grew up in a home where each child was born a stairstep from the other, my older brothers were much older than me; 7 and 11 years older. By the time I was 7, I was an only child in the house. My oldest brother graduated and joined the Air Force, and the other brother was sent off to boarding school for gifted kids in Pennsylvania. At least that's what they told me. I never believed it, though. An anonymous source tipped me off that during those years, he was actually locked up in Spofford (Juvenile Detention Center) in the Bronx, and that didn't seem like the kind of thing my grandmother would lie about. Regardless, I was on my own. I didn't have to share a room with two sweaty teenage boys anymore. I could get in the bathroom to shower and brush my teeth, and taking a dump was no longer a competitive sport to see who could dash to the toilet faster. And I could have what I wanted for dinner. There are tons of benefits to being an only child, and I reaped all that I could. From then on, I had my own everything.

When my brothers left the house, there was way less music in our home, but that Billie Holiday song still echoed in my head. "Mama may have, Papa may have, but God bless the child that's got his own. That's got his own! Them that's strong get more, while the weak ones fade, empty pockets don't ever make the grade; Mama may have, Papa may have, but god bless the child that's got his own. That's got his own!" My brothers took this mantra out into the world. They were serious, both serving in the Armed Forces and going on to have their own families at a young age. They never reached back for anything. The middle brother even graduated "Spofford " early, going on to graduate college at 20 years old before becoming a commissioned officer in the Marines. All the while, in their absence, I was spreading out on the beds they left at home in the room that was finally all mine.

I was a quiet kid. I didn't go out and interact that much with other kids. I simply walked to school in the morning and back home in the afternoon. Every teacher in the school knew who I was because my parents had both been PTA president. Plus, my two older brothers both attended the school before me. I even had some of the same teachers. I was either known by the teachers as Mr. and Mrs. Reid's son or Dez and Dwayne's brother. I never actually had my own identity. Turns out that I had to share that with my brothers even though they were gone.

Now I understand how my dad felt about his sister's shoes. I don't think a lot of teachers in the school even knew my first name. In kindergarten and first grade, there was another kid with the same name as me. Whenever we were addressed by the teacher or by other students, either the letter "B" or the letter "R" was said after our first name in order to distinguish us from one another. The only saving grace was that SHE didn't follow me to the same second-grade class. From there on, I at least knew that when my name was mentioned, I was the one being addressed. It wasn't until college, when I moved to Atlanta, that I was free of being known as just my parents' kid or my brothers' brother, and I was simply Dane. It felt good.

My freshman year in college, I reveled in this. I said my name as much as I could. "Hi, I'm Dane Reid," never simply just Dane. I wanted to brand my identity. I said it to people as if I were famous. And I had a famous-sounding name, so it worked. Girls seemed to like it. I met a lot of girls by looking them in the eyes, gently shaking their hands and saying my name. And a lot of them ended up saying my name too, very loudly and repeatedly while they panted and called out the lord's name in vain in short succession. At that point, even the neighbors knew my name.

By my sophomore year, I met a girl who I liked so much that I wanted to give her my last name. I was crazy about her, and she was crazy about me, so I made her my girlfriend. But just a few months into the relationship, people stopped asking me, "How are you?" and skipped immediately to "How is Tiffenie?" I lost my identity again. There were times that I really wanted to just be me. I regained it for a few years when I dated Brittany simply because all of my friends hated her, but I lost it again when I met my next girlfriend.

As I got older and observed parents having kids, I noticed a similar trend. When I worked in the school system, parents were known by their kids' names. This was a huge change from what I grew up experiencing. I thought that maybe, just maybe, if I decided to have kids one day, I would be known as Dane, and my kid would be known as Dane's son. But society had been flipped on its head. In is out. Left is right. And kids now overshadow their parents.

When you become a parent, you're invisible, only relevant to your child's existence. I struggled with that my entire life, only being recognized for my relationship to someone else. My parents, my siblings, my girlfriends, had all overshadowed my existence. When I see my friend's experience within the context of just being a parent and being ignored for their own wellbeing, I wonder, "Is that your whole purpose in life? Are you just Hailey's Dad now?" I want to be me. I want to live for myself. I want my own pair of shoes. I want my own fork again, my own seat at the table, and for people to ask how I am doing. I like having to consider myself and for others to genuinely be concerned with my wellbeing.

My friend Ben has four daughters. He's had to learn to pee sitting down just so he doesn't forget to put the toilet seat down, a punishable offense in his house which lands him in the "No Penetration Penitentiary" by his wife, Jessica. I've told Ben many times to stand up for his rights and enforce the gender-neutral position rule for the toilet bowl. This way, everyone has to put down both the seat and the lid. Ask any plumber: open toilets are nasty. When your toilet flushes, it's like it just sneezed shit all over the bathroom. When Ben found that out, he started crapping in the kids' bathroom, where their toothbrushes were exposed to his fecal blast. He's outnumbered in that house and has to resort to passive-aggressive measures to feel any sense of power. But even that backfired because he was the one who had to spend nine hours in the E.R. after two of his daughters developed intestinal problems.

Ben can't just do as he pleases. He always has to consider his family, especially the kids. We had planned a guys' trip to the Dominican Republic. Mike and I had been talking to Ben for months about this trip. But two weeks before the trip, Ben pulled out because his daughter had a volleyball tournament the week we were leaving. I joked that maybe if he had learned to "pull out" years ago, he would've been able to go on this trip with us. I had been telling him about my famous "Quick Withdraw McGraw" method. He said he tried it, but obviously, it failed him four times. Now he's paying for it.

It seemed as if every time we wanted to do something, one of the kids got sick, or had an activity, or something inconvenient came up. Even when his kids got to their teens, we couldn't plan anything with Ben. I remember the night of our friend Darnell's bachelor party. It was set to be wild. Ben was supposed to bring the alcohol but didn't come because he got the call that his oldest daughter Benji had driven off the road. It turned out that she fell asleep at the wheel.

And it wasn't just our vacations either. Ben had wanted to take his wife on vacation and asked me where he should take her. By then, I had been all over the world and knew lots of great spots. I suggested Roatan, Honduras. He and Jessica did all their research on it and were excited and booked their tickets. But at the last minute, Jessica's mother, who was supposed to watch the kids the week they were gone, canceled. There was no explanation, but none was needed. She's free from raising kids and may have simply decided not to watch them. She was being selfish, and that's her right.

In a last-ditch effort to salvage their vacation, Ben asked me to babysit for a week. You can imagine the look I gave him when he broached that question. It was followed by a laugh, an eye roll, and a "GTFOH! Are you crazy?" Even though I often felt bad for him, I couldn't help Ben out. I just couldn't! Ben had miscalculated what his life would be like with kids, and I wasn't going to let him subtract from my peace.

If I had agreed to watch Ben's kids while he and Jessica were gone, where would I have even watched them? At my house? No way! Ben's rowdy ass kids weren't allowed at my house. And I couldn't go to his house because I work from my home studio. I need quietness to do my job. I'd hate to have to yell "STFU" at his kids while I'm recording, but I would.

I remember when I was looking for a house. Ben and Jessica were looking at the same time, and we had the same realtor, Keith. My requirements were simple. I needed two bedrooms and a space where I could record voiceovers for work. It needed to be nice, but that was it. Ben and Jessica had greater considerations. They were already in a home, but they had outgrown it (and let the kids destroy it) and needed more space. Keith found me a home within two months. It took him nearly eleven months to find a home for Ben and Jessica. This was largely because they had a laundry list of requirements.

Ben and Jessica wanted a nice home, but they also had to make sure that it was in a good school district with a great volleyball program, had enough bedrooms and bathrooms for all the kids, was near a playground, and wasn't too far from Jessica's mother's house. After eleven months, Keith convinced them to take a house that had most of their needs. It was far from Jessica's mother's house, which

Ben considered a blessing and a curse. While Ben would avoid the unwanted surprise visits by his mother and law, he now had to drive extra far after work to pick up the kids from her house.

The other issue was that they moved to a district that didn't have a championship volleyball team. Ben and Jessica bet big on their kids' future playing college volleyball, and now that future was in jeopardy. To solve that problem, Jessica rented an apartment in their old neighborhood for $1600 per month just so Benji could continue playing for that school. That worked for about a year before the cops came knocking on their door. Jessica nearly caught a case. Personally, I think Ben set her up, but that's a story for another book.

Ben and Jessica gave up a lot of themselves and their desires for one thing: their kids. And they didn't even seem happy. They moved far away to the burbs, where they had to travel an hour just to meet up with their friends, and that's just the few times when they could get away from the kids. They spent outrageous amounts of loot on their kids instead of doing things to salvage their own sanity. Their marriage almost failed several times. And Jessica almost ended up in jail. I knew them both before they were parents to teen and tween girls, and they were cool and selfish people. We were the selfish crew, doing whatever we wanted. But when the girls came along, I became the outlier. Not in thought, but in practice.

This all seemed insane. Life was fine, in fact, great, before they became parents. Had Jessica's mother not warned her how hard raising kids would be? Even I warned them. Well, I warned Ben. They gave up so much of what they loved in life. I like to keep what I got and keep getting more. Lots of people call me selfish for not having children, a logic that I don't get. Instead, I think it's selfish to have the children and then stress out the entire family because you now have to sacrifice things you didn't want to. Children feel those emotions, and it affects them. I think it's selfish to give life and not give it your all. I think it's selfish to make such a big decision without truly considering what you're getting into. If not doing that to myself, my partner and my kids is selfish, then so be it. I guess I'm selfish, and that's okay.

Chapter 10
Reason #268
I Am Not a Role Model

In 1993 Nike rolled the dice and released a series of ads featuring Charles Barkley stating, "I am not a role model. I am not paid to be a role model. I am paid to wreak havoc on the basketball court" (Luke-Norris, 2020). Barkley went on to declare, "Parents should be role models" (Mehdi, 2021). These words shocked the parenting world. For many years, celebrities were hailed as the pillars of good behavior and role models, and parents just pointed at them and told their kids, "See him? Do that." But Barkley broke the mold, and Nike amplified his on- and off-court antics by using him in these controversial ads. Here was a guy who spat at another player, missed and hit a woman, who spent five days in jail for a DUI and who threw a man through a window, and yet parents were mad because he didn't want to be their kids' hero.

Nike and Barkley were telling the truth. Celebrities aren't there to raise kids. They are there to be celebrities. That doesn't indemnify them from their bad behavior and subsequent influence. They just shouldn't be used to indemnify parents from being neglectful of their own children.

Parents, too, are guilty of bad behavior. They forget the adage, "monkey see, monkey do." Or they just don't care. Either way, and whether parents like it or not, those little monkeys are like sponges. From birth to age three, a child unconsciously absorbs more information than at any point in their lives, and that hyper-learning by observation doesn't stop there (Maunz, n.d.). That poses problems for many parents who aren't willing or able to shake their bad habits. Even habits and actions parents are unaware of are being picked up on and stored by their children. Children save your subtle mannerisms, your speech pattern and accent, the way you walk, and yes, the things you do and say all on their organic hard drives, ready to be recalled and mimicked without warning (Steber, 2018). You are never safe to be an unfiltered adult if your goal is to raise a filtered child.

My parents were careful about what they did, but they couldn't completely combat the influence of the streets. The result was that I grew up way more hardcore than most kids do now. If you didn't hear cursing in your house from your parents, your friends or your older siblings, then you weren't living in Brooklyn. There was no way our parents could shield us from the outside world. But in an era of parental controls on devices where parents hold their 19-year-old's hand to cross the street, these soft-ass kids nowadays think "lie" is a bad word. They think "stupid" is the S-word. I'll tell you what starts with the letter "S" and is a lie, but their parents say it to them anyway: Santa. The F-word in that scenario is "Fraud." The "F" word in my time was "Fuck."

Growing up, too often I heard other kids' parents cursing at them. I had grown so used to my parents being squeaky clean that the one time my dad told me to "Get off my DAMN butt and do something," I was ready to call BCW (Bureau of Child Welfare) for child abuse. Our home was a bubble, but I was still well prepared for the outside world, filled with F-bombs and MF-bombs. That outside influence was powerful. In my neighborhood, other kids in my school started cursing as early as Kindergarten, but not me. I at least had the decency to hold off until first grade. My parents raised me right.

I remember testing the waters. At five years old, I had heard someone on TV say hell. Hell, I heard the preacher in church say hell. Hell was everywhere except in my house. So I dragged it in from the street one time and used it in a sentence in front of my older brother. Guess who reported it to my mother as if it was CNN Breaking News. My brother. By the time it reached my mother's ears, I had been practicing my technique on how to best absorb the slap I was about to get. If only she had given me more time. She immediately called me into the kitchen and told me to never use those kinds of words again. She even included a live action demonstration of what would happen to me if I did, followed up by time out.

I learned to steer clear of dirty words. That was until Georgie. Georgie was a kid in my neighborhood who obviously didn't get the five-finger memo that my mother sent out. He was a tough kid who said the F-word first thing when he woke up in the morning. Plus, he liked to fight. I found out about Georgie's relationship with the F-word the hard way. One day in first grade, we were in the schoolyard playing handball, and Georgie and I collided with one another while chasing after the ball. Georgie, being the confrontational guy he was, got upset and got in my face and pushed me. Other kids quickly intervened, but Georgie was intent on fighting and was trying his best to break away from them, at one point even throwing a kick that almost struck me. I wasn't gonna take that. He started dropping F-bombs on me, and I had nothing to shoot them down with. Imagine me fending him off by saying, "DON'T USE THOSE DIRTY WORDS, YOU BAD BAD BULLY!" That would've gotten my ass kicked. It was at that moment that I decided to arm myself with the same tools that the enemy had. I wasn't allowed to say "Hell" like the preacher did, but just like the preacher when they brought those sex allegations against him, I would let no weapon formed against me prosper. I belted out a string of profanities at Georgie that would influence my vocabulary for the rest of my days. I told that little piece of shit, "FUCK YOU MOTHERFUCKER! I'LL FUCK YOU UP!" plus more stuff that I don't remember. I was in a zone. My tirade lasted what seemed like hours and when I was done, Georgie backed down. It was then I realized the utility of cursing. I never turned back.

Over time, I began to enjoy it. My mother taught me not to curse. The streets taught me to curse, just not around adults I knew. I learned to switch it off at home, but in school, like all the kids, I cursed like a sailor. I even heard my teachers cursing in casual conversations with each other. They didn't know our little ears could intercept them. Cursing was as ubiquitous in elementary school as people throwing up after eating school lunch. Over the years, cursing wasn't just what I did, it was a part of who I was. My mother claims that one day when I was a teen, it was reported to her that someone heard me in the street cursing and had no idea that such a nice young man from such a good home would use such bad language. By the time my mother brought it to my attention, I was grown, and we got a good laugh out of it. Plus, I had learned how to block by then.

It's not just what we say that makes a difference in raising children, it's also what we do. It's often the small things that we don't even notice that other people, including children, observe. Lamar Odem, I'm sure, wishes Nike would give him an "I am not a role model" commercial. After Lamar was caught on camera scratching his nuts during his post-performance interview on "Dancing With The Stars," there was outrage and condemnation. What was he supposed to do, just let them itch? Was ABC supposed to blur out his hand and junk as he reached to relieve his formication? I guess they figured Justin Timberlake got away with revealing Janet Jackson's boobs on live television, so what's a little jock itch. But people didn't see it that way. They joked about Lamar, and some on Twitter invoked his influence over kids.

I see a lot of things wrong with this. Firstly, why is a former coke-addicted guy who married a Kardashian an influence on your kids? Secondly, who is watching your kids while you are tweeting about Lamar Odem? And lastly, have some compassion for the guy. He could've been having an outbreak, and the urge to scratch was too great. It's not like he was bouncing your kid on his lap at the mall and promising him rewards if he is "a good boy." That would be creepy. And while those Twitter parent punks may be unnecessarily outraged over Odem's irritation, I get the sentiment that you have to have self-awareness in all forums where little eyes could be watching.

I used to work in the school system where hundreds of eyes were always watching. If you ever want to find a place where adults behave badly, find a school where there are both men and women teaching. Not only are the teachers freaks, but parents also join in on it too. I had more than a few unorthodox parent-teacher conferences with moms. Most took place outside of school, but a few mothers insisted on meeting inside the classroom. Horny mothers do the least to hide their actions from their kids. I was nearly caught by one of the kindergarten students I worked with while doing a home visit with his mother. He had no idea I was even in the house. Luckily, I heard him coming. By the time he walked in the living room, I had jumped behind the sofa to hide. Imagine if I had been caught with my junk in his mother. I could've been fired. Ironically, his grandmother worked in the same school as I did and did get fired for doing the same thing with a married coworker in one of the classrooms.

One reason I don't want to be a parent is that I love having loud sex. I mean REALLY loud sex. I love having "Someone call 911 because this lady is being murdered" loud sex. As a single guy, sex with me was always a community event. It was like a loud, hard-hitting, four-quarter Superbowl matchup where the fans cheered us on from their own apartments. Sometimes, my neighbors even served as cheerleaders. The entire event was as big as the halftime show, except with me running the plays, there was no intermission. The neighbors knew my name long before Trey Songz wrote his hit song. He got the idea from me. Raping women though? He invented that himself.

Sex didn't always happen at my house. Sometimes women wanted to hook up but couldn't find a babysitter. Normally in these situations, I had to sneak into their houses during the middle of the night while the kid was sleeping. Other times I would come by the woman's house while the kid was awake and wait around until the kids went to bed before I could spend some adult time with mommy. Then there were also the times when mommy would plop her little one in front of the TV or video game while she took me into her room to play with my joystick. I dated one woman who used that trick one too many times. After a year of dating her, her 12-year-old finally figured out why his mommy and I always disappeared during "Call of Duty."

It was during my twenties that I became an actual motherfucker. But fucking mothers wasn't as fun and action-packed as fucking non-mothers. Motherfucking was noticeably quieter. Fucking mothers required being able to satisfy a woman who measured my strokes by how little the bed squeaked. I had to learn to gauge a woman's enjoyment solely by the scrunch of her face without the help of an audible sound. I had to be the lookout person in the bank robbery and the guy who passes the note to the teller so as not to cause a scene. This was more like the Masters than the Superbowl. I still had to maintain par and win but couldn't bring all the fans onto the course to cheer. In this game, there were more potential interruptions, it's a lot quieter and usually less fun to play.

It's hard to hide things from kids. Even when a parent does everything right in front of their children, they still have to be careful. Parents have to conceal their actions and their possessions because kids like to discover things that weren't intended for children to find. Once, Ben and Jessica's kids found mommy's rabbit in her drawer and thought it was a toy rocket ship. Jessica walked in the living room surprised to see Barbie strapped on top of it as she flew around the house. Some kids find sex toys and Playboys that belong to their parents, and while that's bad, it could always be worse. In the United States there are more guns than people and most are unsecured (Hamilton et al., 2018). A friend of mine faced charges in North Carolina when it was discovered that his son found his gun in his unlocked safe. Things could've gone terribly wrong and unfortunately, in too many cases, they do. From accidental home shootings to intentional school shootings, too many children have access to weapons (Anderson & Sabia, 2018). It's just another thing that parents have to keep far away from the hands and eyes of kids.

I continue to monitor my behavior when I am around my family. My parents still don't curse, and I don't curse around any of them. Occasionally when I'm with my family, a bad word slips out in frustration, but not often. Those are times when I'm in the car driving with them, and some asshole cuts me off. Or when I'm cooking at my house with my family there and hot grease shoots out of the frying pan and burns my hand. But what am I supposed to say in those instances? Fiddlesticks? It's just not the same. I love the word "FUCK." It's my favorite English word and has so many uses. It brings me joy saying it.

If I were a dad, I'd have to hold it in. Curious eyes are watching, listening, and processing, ready to repeat every word like a parrot. That's a lot of pressure whenever I am around kids, but to have to maintain that charade 24/7, even in the comfort of my own house, would be impossible. I live alone in an environment tailor-made for adult conversations, adult actions and anti-role modeling. It's a place to drop my guard and unload the stress of the outside world. Where would I go if the stress was being compounded by the little people living in my house? I would be trapped, and the worst part about it is I couldn't even collect rent from them.

Chapter 11
Reason # 33
Who's Gonna Entertain Them?

In my late teens and early twenties, I went out on a lot of dates. I would take girls out to eat at restaurants or include them in activities I didn't want to do alone. I would tell them to meet me in these places so we could get to know each other better, but my objective was usually singular: trying to figure out if we could get this horizontal hockey game going. I didn't know what I was going to talk about with them. I figured I would compliment them by telling them how pretty they were and flirt with them a lot. If I felt bold enough, I would say something nasty to them or touch them in a way that sexually excited them. My objective, quite simply, was sex.

When you're young, you know that what you have most in common with a young woman is raging hormones. You may have other things in common, but that's the one we're pretty sure about from the time we express interest in one another. Oh, and the fact that we're not sure about anything else. I used to take these young women on dates with little else to talk about. Often after I asked a girl her favorite color and what her college major was, there was an awkward silence. We weren't experienced at communication, and worse, we had little to no life experience to draw from.

As I got older, this became easier. I was able to talk to women about jobs, health, past relationships, moving from city to city, life objectives, etc., and the conversations gelled. We had more thoughts and memories and cultural references to pool from, plus an understanding from interacting with other people. It was so much more than just baiting women with how enormous my penis is. It was baiting them with how vast my knowledge was *and* how enormous my penis is. I was able to connect with women on a more profound level, which made sex, even when they were just hookups, feel deeper.

Once I reached my mid-30s, it was game over. I knew enough, met enough people, had enough experiences, hung out with celebrities, knew enough jokes, ate at the best restaurants, and knew enough pop culture references to keep a conversation going all night. Impressively enough, I could even chat it up while kissing a woman's thighs, unhooking her bra with one hand, and pulling her dress over her head all at the same time. The way I worked my mouth and appendages simultaneously, you would think my mother was an orator, and my dad was Inspector Gadget. I could Go Go gadget conversation all the way up until the post-ejaculatory nap. In my 30s, I had a lot to say to women.

Traveling changed my world and expanded what I had to offer to a conversation. I didn't just travel to bask in the sunlight and sip margaritas. I traveled in basic economy to places where the economies were poor, but the experiences and stories were rich. I met and spoke with people who told me their stories of suffering, struggling, and overcoming. Those people and their stories gave me things to think about and bring back to the United States, and in turn, I shared them with other Americans. People contributed something valuable to conversations wherever I went. They challenged my understanding and beliefs, and I loved it. I loved talking about more than what their favorite color was and what their major in college was.

It was around this time that my interest in women changed, too. Being pretty wasn't enough to attract me in the way that it had been in my 20s. I began looking at women for what they contributed to conversations. I had become a sapiosexual who often turned down dates with a "Hot Chick" after the first boring conversation. I needed more. I began noticing a difference when I dated women who were my age as opposed to women in their 20s. Other men I knew didn't want their dates to be smart, but I had graduated from that mindset. I didn't want a pet. I wanted a partner.

My mid-thirties was also the time when conversations about having children began to peak. People around me wanted to know more and more about whether I would ever reproduce. I was pretty sure the answer was no, but I left the door open for something incredibly compelling to change my mind. Aside from all the things that I would have to sacrifice to have children, there was one thing I was unwilling to give up. Actually, there were dozens of things, but for the purpose of this chapter, I'm only talking about one. It was the intellectual exchange that I had grown used to in grown-up conversation.

There is always an awkward silence between me and kids anytime I try to engage in conversation with them. It's reminiscent of those dates in my early twenties when I didn't know what to say. And unless I'm trying to score with the kid's mama, I don't even know what my objective is. Usually, I talk to kids about the same things I talked about with girls in their twenties. The conversations start and end with, "So how is school?" and "What do you want to be when you get older?" Even when I have extended chats with kids, I'm the only one sharing, and they're the only ones potentially benefiting from the conversation. I say potentially because I usually feel like I'm lecturing and that they totally can't relate, in which case I have to ask the $100 question: "Why the fuck are we talking?"

That may seem harsh, but I don't have anything to trade with kids. Lots of my friends get down on the floor and huddle around their kids' reinforced tablets to watch Cocomelon with them. I'm not doing that. Who's gonna help me get up? The kid? No, they're too busy being mesmerized by a fly flying across the screen back and forth and watermelon with a face chasing its own tail while some kid yells out, "Cocomelon!" This is entertaining? If you ever want to see toddlers lose their minds, play the theme song to Cocomelon and watch what happens. It's incredible to watch. Not the show, the reaction. The show itself has no value to anyone without kids except for the creators who are raking in the YouTube ad bucks. I'm neither entertained nor raking in the dough.

I'm not the guy who gets kids' songs and movies stuck in my head, either. I hear parents singing kids songs all the time as if it's the newest Drake jam. They say they don't talk about Bruno, yet they still go around town singing about him. I don't get it. Lin-Manuel Miranda and I attended the same High School at the same time, but just like in High School Spanish class, I fell asleep during Encanto. It just wasn't enchanting. And in what universe of adults would Yo Gabba Gabba's Party in My Tummy get 62 million views? I'll answer that. Only the universe where parents exist. My friend Candace, who has three daughters, told me that at one time, tickets to a Yo Gabba Gabba concert (yes, that was a real thing) started at $100. Do you know how many Miami flights on Spirit that is? My poor kid would be stuck watching our friendly neighbor Mr. Rogers sing creepy educational songs. I'm not paying $100 for a kids' concert. I'm going to Miami.

The only Gabba I want in my life is a good gab with a good friend. That's always been hard for me to have with anyone significantly younger. I can't use adult humor around them or curse, which is some real bullshit. I can't be myself, and I'm not getting value. I want to talk about the time I finally made it to Machu Picchu and got terribly sick and was separated from my buddies. Or the time I flew 30 hours to the other side of the globe to hang out with some guys I met once in an airport. I want to talk about the time my nerdy friend Ross told me that he was in a whorehouse in Medellin with his pants down when the "policia" busted in to make sure there were no underage workers there. That's not the kind of story he could've told me if we were around minors. He said he thought he was gonna go to jail. It was a much more interesting Colombian story than anything Lin-Manuel has ever released. Ross had me in stitches. But every time a kid tells me a story about something they saw on TV, in a movie or online, I laugh as much as I do when my internet service is interrupted.

I played with toys and watched movies as a kid too. I especially liked He-Man and She-Ra action figures. These kids don't have half the imagination I did when I was their age. My He-Man used to do some crazy stuff with his sword when She-Ra was around. These kids have Beyblade instead, where they spin two jagged-edged, space-aged-looking dreidels around in a circular plastic box to see which one disintegrates after ramming into the other. I did something similar with He-Man, but She-Ra never disintegrated. She-Ra withstood the abuse.

There are shows, commentary by YouTubers, and tournaments involving these Beyblade toys. But to me, predicting the winner is as easy as observing the speed of the Beyblade and which one was spun into the ring first. Usually, that's the one that loses. It's simple physics. Kids don't get that. They think it has something to do with the ridges on the edges of the toys. But forget explaining probability to a kid who drinks the Kool-Aid from YouTube videos. Every time a child explains to me Beyblade using kid logic, I lose my mind. I simply can't come down to that level and just enjoy it for being mindless fun.

That makes me appreciate my parents even more, who came down to my level when I was a kid. I remember my dad taking me out to the driveway a few times when I was younger and throwing the ball around with me. My dad was a huge baseball fan back in the day, and I shared his love for the sport. I was in elementary school back then, and I loved all things baseball. During Phys. Ed, I was always so excited to play wiffle ball. After school, I threw a tennis ball at a target on a wall while wearing my baseball glove whenever I could. Sometimes I would throw it at different parts of the wall and chase it down to test my reflexes as if I were on the field. I liked the infield, especially pitcher and first base. I never had a thing for the catcher's position, though. It was too tough of a job.

Mostly, I played by myself, and as I got older, I don't remember playing with my dad at all. As a parent with a small kid, it's much easier to chase your little Rickey Hendersons around the backyard. But as your child becomes more Rickey Henderson than even Ricky Henderson is now, it becomes harder to keep up. They require a larger field, a stronger arm, faster legs, and the ability to jump, dive, and get back up again. Out of the six things that I just named, I only have one of those things: a larger field. I don't know how many of those my dad had, but I know he had far less time and energy after work to explore those things with me.

So the solution was to put me on a losing softball team that met every Saturday in Prospect Park in Brooklyn. I don't think they intentionally put me on a losing team, but I don't remember my self-esteem being higher while heading home after any of the eight games I played. After that summer, all I could remember is not wanting to play anymore. Maybe that was the plan all along. My dad is a smart guy. Perhaps he plotted to discourage me from wanting to play with him anymore, so he didn't have to throw, jump, dive and get back up again.

I don't blame him. My dad is 32 years older than me. When I was 10, he was at the age where most guys are calling the shots from the sidelines, not getting muddy on the field. Instead of crashing against the outfield wall to steal a home run, they're using their brains. But when you work as hard as my parents did, and still do, who has extra innings left in their brains to concoct plays from the sidelines? My parents were involved in a lot of things, and sometimes throwing the ball around was sidelined by other more immediate things.

Even when my dad had time to share his love of baseball, it was for the New York Mets. I, on the other hand, was a fan of their crosstown rival Yankees. The Yankees had a storied history and just appealed to me more. They had more interesting characters, from the aforementioned Rickey Henderson to Don Mattingly to Derek Jeter and Mariano Rivera. The Mets just had players who wished they were Yankees—people like Darryl Strawberry. My Dad couldn't bring himself to watch the Bronx Bombers, so he tried his hardest to get me to switch. Nope! It wasn't happening. It never happened. Even though we both loved the game, we seldom watched them together because we just didn't like each other's team. We were so close to having something in common, but the Interborough rivalry kept us apart.

The one time I remember my bat rising for the same team as my dad's was when I was seven, and my father took me to the movies to see "Revenge of The Nerds." Maybe he thought "Rated R" meant that the movie was "REALLY GOOD" as opposed to "Rated G," which was just "Good." If so, you can't fault my dad for wanting to give me the best. I was excited about this flick, but I couldn't wait till next time for him to take me to see an X-tra good movie. There we were in the theater watching these nerds invading a sorority house, or whatever the hell was happening, when all those boobs began flying across the screen like a ladybug. That movie exposed me to coco melons long before YouTube existed. I had never seen exposed breasts in a movie theater before. ET didn't have them. Neither did Star Wars. But these nerds had them. As the knockers busted out of their shirts, I looked over at my dad to see if it was okay to keep watching. My dad was expressionless, as if the breasts weren't even there. He couldn't control what was on the screen, so he played it completely cool, and at that moment, I felt like he had climbed down on the floor and huddled around the tablet with me.

I could never show my theoretical seven-year-old movies with naked breasts in them. He'd have to find them the old-fashioned way: from my open computer tabs. We'd just have to bond on another level. Maybe he'd like Chipotle as much as I do. I'd have to hope that when he grows up, we could chat it up about the Yankees, Miami nights, 30-hour flights, and nerds in whorehouses in Colombia. But that will never happen, because I couldn't stay awake through a seven-year-old's movie.

Chapter 12
Reason #101
I Don't Find Kids Interesting

I don't find kids interesting. Not in the way other people do. I've seen a lot of people who are simply fascinated with children. They get a kick out of all things kids and confidently claim their kids are set apart from the rest. I know better. I have watched children grow: they are not unique. Just like adults, they can be grouped into personality and ability types. Few are Picasso enough to hang their art on my refrigerator. Few are Warren Buffet enough to start their own lemonade business that will move us out of the ghetto. And most aren't as smart as their parents think they are. The attributes parents ogle over in their kids are usually exaggerated by the fish-eyed lenses of love, hope, and delusion that mothers and fathers develop after their first kid is born.

I'm always amazed when I hear parents say about a three-month-old, "Oh, he's so spoiled." Is he? Or is he just three months old and dependent on you for literally everything? This is what I mean. Parents have assigned these fictional characteristics to their kids and actually believe them. Or parents say things like, "She's so smart" because their daughter holds their finger tightly when the parent sticks it out. I should hope she can grasp your finger. For goodness' sake, she's 12. What would be more impressive is if she stopped wetting the bed. Few parents ever pick up a child development book to see that their child is simply on track with the rest or, worse, has completely derailed.

As a parent, you simply don't see flaws in your children. You see greatness. You see the hope of what you never were or never had. You see the possibility that you can be greater through them. But here's a harsh truth: You are not them. They are themselves. And every single one of their peers have parents who equally believe in their own children's greatness. That includes the kid who spat on your kid during lunch. It includes the kid who licked the window on the bus. And it also includes the kid who farts all day during class. By the way, for any of my old classmates reading this book, that was me. I wasn't holding it in for any of you window lickers.

I'm sure my parents smelled my farts at home, just like some of you smell your lactose intolerant kids' stinky butts. Some of you are looking at my past as the room booty bomber and saying, "Well, you turned out okay." You're saying to yourself, "Maybe one day my little man will be a successful voice actor with thousands of projects to his name too." Maybe he will be, but for now, your life stinks, and you're stuck having to laugh it off through 18 years with Farty McFly. If only you could go back to the future when your car wasn't consumed by putrid odors from the car seat in the back. The backseat was where you made that monster of yours. Now, look what's become of it. To cope, parents pretend that this is cute. In fact, everything that their kids do at an early age is cute. Farting, cursing, spitting at other kids, it's all cute because it has to be.

Lots of things that children do are just practice for adulthood. I'm not blown away by watching the growth process just because I get to witness it from the adult perspective. I get it. We were all small once. Think about it. We all entered into a bright world from a dark womb with no knowledge of what the hell we were even brought here for. Childhood to adulthood and even the slow march toward our final breath is all a journey that we can't observe in the third person. Having children who share in our DNA is an opportunity for us to witness what we were like going through those early stages. That can be quite interesting. But for a guy like me, who had great self-awareness as a child, and who spent years around other people's kids, it's not compelling enough to long for a rerun of my younger days.

Kids aren't TV either. I have seen lots of parents use their kids as forms of entertainment. Everything the kid says is funny to them. It gets to a point where the children know that their parent is entertained by them and become dependent on that comedic approval from the parent as the basis for their self-esteem. This works when they are three, four, and five years old. But once the child outgrows the cuddly years and has a mustache, it can be devastating when their parents no longer laugh at their stage shows.

I take having children so seriously that it would be hard for me not to look at them as a project. They aren't entertainment. They aren't pets. They are little people who will spend more time as adults than they will as children. I don't want them wasting time learning to roll over and bark and give me their paws. I want them to learn to paint like Picasso and start the next Berkshire Hathaway. If you start them early with a purpose, they will follow the path. Tiger's dad knew what he wanted his son to be. Venus and Serena's parents had a plan. Golf and Tennis are entertaining, but Earl Woods and Richard Williams weren't entertained by putting in the hard work it took to take their kids to the top of their sports. They were investing in their children's futures because their futures depended on it.

Whether you have a silver spoon to feed them with or not, kids must learn about real life. The window to teach them those things is narrow. You can't wait till they're teens. The time many parents spend fawning over their children's cuteness is the opportune time. After that, they find you as interesting to talk to as you find them cute. I have found myself in conversations with teens who I wonder why I am wasting my breath. I should be on a flight to Maui instead. But as a public service, I try to teach young people the things I learned so they can speed out of the blocks as soon as the gun goes off. Usually, I catch them dozing off or rolling their eyes, and I come off sounding like an old guy. As much as I love teaching people things, I'm not into teaching them things they don't want to learn. While I enjoy working out, I'm not one to exercise my futility.

The life cycle is fun to watch. It's fun to contribute to someone else's experiences, but there is no story more interesting to me than my own. I am successful, so I don't feel like I need to reset my life via someone else. I have a great story to tell. It's a full story from childhood to now, where even the most interesting parts come from adulthood. The fun stuff didn't happen at Barbie's doll house. It happened in the frat house. Those are the things I'm interested in.

Chapter 13
Reason #521
Jeffrey Dahmer Versus MLK

A great American philosopher once said, "Kids are like a box of chocolates. You never know what you're gonna get." And it's true. But while you may think it was Forrest Gump who penned that quote, it wasn't. It was Forrest's father. Most people think about greatness and believe that their kid will be the embodiment of it. "My daughter will be the doctor who cures cancer," they imagine. They reflect on great figures before their time and think, "My son can be like MLK." And it's true. Your son can be like MLK.

Dr. King was a great human rights figure who is admired all around the world. He was key in convincing President Johnson to push for and sign the voting rights act. He was the youngest ever awardee of the Nobel Peace Prize. He organized the Montgomery bus boycotts and encouraged peaceful protest and non-violent resistance to violence. He was a central figure in organizing the march on Washington. And once there, he delivered to the world what is arguably the most powerful speech in history (Dorrien, 2018).

When I was in elementary school, I was chosen to give Dr. King's most famous speech because of my booming voice. Inspired by him, I even looked up in the sky and paused before I uttered the words of his dream for the world. I modeled his mannerisms. Despite never meeting him, I was awestruck by his towering personality and thought, "One day, I want to be like MLK." Martin is an icon, still to this day, although in America, it's partly because he never lived long enough to be the villain.

Meanwhile, on the other side of the auditorium, as I gave my speech, there was another kid, inspired by another famous American. His dream was to be like Jeffrey Dahmer. Okay. Maybe not in my school. I don't know. But there might have been another kid who wanted to eat me for lunch. That kid probably viewed Jeffrey Dahmer, who had become a news obsession for his murder of men and boys he lured into having sex with before killing and eating them, as an antihero. Between 1978 and 1991, Dahmer was known to have killed 17 males (Watts, 2018). By all accounts, he was a nice guy. So much so that he managed to avoid suspicion by police even when he was caught with a naked 14-year-old boy who was running in the streets. Police believed Dahmer when he told them that the boy was 19 and they were just lovers having a spat. The police thought Dahmer to be persuasive enough that they left the scene without investigating further. Dahmer went on to murder the boy and ate him. Dahmer, like King, was murdered, but unlike King, he lived long enough to be a hero.

These two Americans couldn't be more different. If you believe the rumors, while one was a psychopathic homicidal cannibal, it was the other one who really liked eating white women. What they had in common was that they were both Americans. Both born in the land of opportunity to parents who dreamed their sons would be kings. And those parents aren't much different from most. Hope blinds parents to the likelihood that their bundle of joy will be average at best (Austin, 2016). I can just hear someone saying, "Well, what if Martin's family had never had him? Where would America be today?" To which I would reply, "Well, what if Jeffrey's parents wouldn't have had him? Maybe one of the 17 boys or men would've been MLK." History is filled with Jeffrey Dahmers. They aren't all certified psychos, but they are almost certainly people who were born into great hope and innocence. From Ray Ray, who was selling drugs outside of the local bodega, to Officer Nice Guy, who was shaking Ray Ray down for his cut of the drug money, there are a lot of bad guys out there. And then there are a lot of people who are simply "meh." But when people think about reproducing, they think about Ahmed who owns the grocery store or Columbo who cracks the case and figures out Officer Nice Guy is crooked.

You just can't predict how kids will turn out. Even kids raised in the same household can turn out differently. Maybe one kid got a full scholarship to a great university and graduated college at 20. So you figure all you need to do is press the repeat button. Unbeknownst to you, in the heat of the moment and dark of night, you hit the skip button and your next child ended up repeating 7th-grade math six times. While your first child is trusted by the government with top secret documents and helps to solve the world's problems, your younger kid is 23 years old and still counts on his fingers. You just never know what variables play into their differences. Order of birth, the state of your relationship with the other parent, the parent's age and more are just some of the things that influence who we become.

One motivation for people having children is that they think that the child is gonna be just like them. That would be great if everyone had a PhD like Dr. King. But unfortunately, the Dunning Krueger effect is a real thing, and most of us are as dumb as Martian rocks. We all have those conversations with people who think they are really smart, or really good-looking or talented, and think, "You really shouldn't pass on those genes." And then you see their kids and realize you were right. Some people who think they are Kings are instead the court jesters. Their only resemblance to royalty is that they seem to be a product of inbreeding.

People are disillusioned to believe they can control the gender of their kids. I was in the park one day when I saw a nice young interracial couple. I could tell from afar that the mother REALLY wanted a girl, and the father put all his hopes in having a boy. They invited all their friends and family to the park to witness them shoot off a confetti cannon. If the confetti was pink, then it was a girl. If it was blue, then dad would have his boy to throw the ball around with and teach him how to hunt and fish. When dad shot that thing off into the air, there was a huge reaction from the crowd. Even strangers were congratulating the ecstatic mother. It was pink. Dad was left looking upset, wishing he had shot something different off. Meanwhile, I was thinking that this whole gender reveal could've gone even worse. If he had fired off that confetti cannon and hit a helicopter, the only boys he would've been concerned about would've been the boys in blue from Homeland security.

I have a friend who wants to have a son. Because of his complicated relationship with his ex-wife, he has no semblance of a relationship with his daughter who is now in her mid-teens. He had a great relationship with his own father and admires the relationships of fathers and sons that he personally knows. The only problem is that at close to 50 years old, he may no longer be firing Y-chromosomes. What happens if he has another daughter? Does he love her any less? Does he keep trying until he gets a boy? And just because he gets a boy doesn't mean that his son won't end up eating white women.

Chapter 14
Reason #71
Not All Kids Are Smart, Not All Kids Are Cute

Remember that scene from Forrest Gump where Jenny tells Forrest that he has a son? Forrest had a rush of emotions, thoughts, and concerns, and the first question he asked was, "Is he smart?" What Forrest really meant was, "Is he smart like me?" Luckily for Little Forrest, he wasn't smart like his dad and instead was *actually* smart, or at least seemingly normal. Forrest had a skewed sense of reality. His self-awareness plagued him throughout the film, putting him in the middle of some of history's most tragic events. This culminated in hoping and believing he had passed on his family's long history of the Einstein gene. Forrest, in thinking this way, isn't alone.

I've met few people who don't believe that they are both smart and attractive. But like in Forrest Gump, the history-making tragic event is when they turn that belief into action and decide to procreate. I think the perception of attractiveness and intelligence often come from people interacting solely in small, insular communities. They only deal with people who look like them, think like them and live like them, so there is never anyone to tell them anything different. There is no one to challenge their ideas. I've met several people who believe the earth is flat and who think they are ultra-intelligent. Those same in-humans passed on their "dumb people who think they are ultra-smart" genetics to people who will also pass them on.

Case in point. I used to be an afterschool and substitute teacher. I did that job for several years, and I saw it all. One of the head-scratching incidents I recall well involved a boy named Kenny. His name was really Kenneth, but he went by Kenny. Kenny was a second grader and was in another after-school teacher's class. He had wanted to go on a school outing to the Teacher's Museum but couldn't get his parents to sign the permission slip.

One day, I reported to the cafeteria where we collected our students each day. They ate snacks and talked before we took them outside to play and then did homework. Out of the corner of my eye, I saw three teachers, one who was Kenny's school day teacher, another his after-school teacher, and the third, the P.E. teacher. They were huddled around Kenny. It was a strange scene. I could tell that they were all trying to contain their laughter but really needed to convey the gravity to Kenny of whatever it was that he had done.

I turned and observed the situation. The P.E. teacher, knowing how tough I often was on the boys in the school, called me over. I walked over, not knowing what I was getting myself into. The P.E. teacher explained what was going on as Little Kenny was drawn close to tears. "Mr. Reid, take a look at this permission slip." As you have probably guessed by now, second-grade Kenny decided that he was going to forge his dad's signature to go on the class trip with the other students. But what was more outrageous, the P.E. teacher explained, was that Kenny handwrote the permission slip after he was denied being able to go and after his parents kept the original copy. Kenny looked at me with fear and regret. I looked at him with great disappointment. "Go sit over there Kenny while I talk this over with your teachers," I grumbled at him with my intimidating voice.

Kenny was probably thinking, "Oh shit, Mr. Reid is gonna kill me and then hand my body over to my dad so he can kill me again." He dragged his little defeated body to the other side of the cafeteria to await our verdict. What he didn't know was that I had been reading the faces of the other teachers, who couldn't hold in their laughter any longer. They tried their best to be serious, but as soon as Kenny was far enough away, they let it all out. I was guilty too. You know how kids do funny things, so you laugh at what they did? This was not that. This was a situation where we were making fun of Kenny. I held the letter in my left hand, poking fun at how he had scribbled the entire thing in pencil. His handwriting was atrocious.

We thought it was hilarious that he really thought he was so clever as to get away with this. As I read some of the funniest parts aloud, I observed something that none of the other teachers had. Prompted by my observation, I pretended to be serious and called Kenny back. The other teachers were curious about my next move, but I didn't let on. Kenny dragged himself back over to us, already looking defeated. I asked him, "Kenny, you signed your dad's name here, didn't you?" Knowing he was caught, he confessed, "Yes," as one tear finally dropped. "And Kenny, you and your dad have the same name, Kenneth, correct?" Again he said, "Yes." I paused, looked up at my colleagues, who too, wondered where this line of questioning was going, then looked down at Kenny again. "Then Kenny, how is it that you still managed to spell it wrong?"

As soon as I said that to Kenny, the other teachers, unable to contain themselves, quickly excused themselves from the conversation. It was as if they had heard the punchline at a Chris Rock show and fallen out of their seats. They were done.

Kenny wasn't the smartest kid in the class. In fact, he represented the lower end of intelligence in his grade. But that doesn't mean he was alone. The funny thing is that when Big Kenny was naming his son on the day he was born, he just knew he had something special. His boy was gonna grow up and be a doctor, or a lawyer or even president someday. And maybe he will. Certainly, in my lifetime, there have been two extremely low intelligent Presidents. All Little Kenny had to do was either buy himself a baseball team and become Governor, or grab one of the teachers by the "P-word," and he was a shoo-in for commander-in-chief. Big Kenny wouldn't have passed on his name if he had known his son would have had too many yards between the goalpost. Poor little Kenny. The wheel kept spinning even though the hamster was dead.

Plenty of children aren't smart, but some parents rave about them as if they are. I just roll my eyes. Having worked with kids for years, I tend to observe things in children that teachers use to judge kids' intelligence. The only kids who were 24 cents short of a quarter and really knew it were the children of teachers. Teachers weren't afraid to tell their kids they weren't "on grade level." I also judge kids on the old timer's scale. I look at where I was at that age and try to project outward 30 years to predict if they might still be stuck in neutral by then. That may not be fair, though. I was exceptionally intelligent as a child. I didn't get great grades, but my dad Dane Sr. assured me that I was still the smartest kid in my school.

Years later, when Kenny was an adult, he found me on social media. He first asked if I remembered him. I told him I did and inquired how he was doing. He told me that he was doing fine. Then he attempted to rehash the past and questioned me laughing at him and doubting his intelligence way back when. He had an ax to grind with me. Kenny went on to tell me more about his newly found success in the face of all odds. I was happy for him. He said he found a trade where he made great money. I asked him what he did for a living. He said he trades his blood plasma for cash. I face-palmed. Little Kenny had not changed.

Just like not all kids are smart, not all kids are cute and attractive. I agree that there is something about small children that really draws you in. Sometimes when I see small kids, I'm left in awe, thinking, "We all started off that small." It's kinda incredible. In my travels, I have seen babies of all flavors and sizes. From Asian babies to African babies and everything in between, if you're not awestruck by what nature has created, then you're cold as a hooker's heart. Truthfully, you're way colder than that, considering many hookers are only hookers because they have babies at home to support. At least that's what they've always told me before asking for a "propina."

English speakers, look it up. That all being said, not all of them are a bundle of visual joy.

We all know that older adults are especially suckers for kids. I think about what they always say when they see babies. I often hear, "Oh, what a cute baby!" Or "Oh, she's so adorable!" Old people often comment on children's looks. "He's so handsome!" But whenever a kid is ugly, you'll notice the change in the language. For example, if the baby is very unattractive, like a 6 on a scale of 1-10, an older person might instead say, "Oh, he's got such bright eyes." A kid that's only a 5 would get, "Oh, how precious she is." But it's all downhill from there. Fours get, "Oh, I'm so happy for you." Threes get, "Oh, when are you having your next one?" Almost to imply, "Better luck next time." Kids that are a 2 get a hesitation before their looks are compared to that of a family member, "Oh, he looks just like his dad's grand-uncle Freddie." That's the same Grand-Uncle that used to haunt people in their dreams. And if the child is a 1, the senior will simply hold the child out with extended arms with their face frowned up and turned away from the kid as if the baby just made stinky. If they say anything at all, it might be just "Oh." Old people don't like to lie. If it's a very old senior, usually a man, he might just say what he's thinking "Your baby looks like he was struck by the back of a garbage truck." Old cranky men have no filter.

Luckily for my mom, she's not an old cranky man. My mother knows a lot of my college friends. She asks about them sometimes, "How's Ben? How are the kids doing?" or "Where is Mike now? Have you spoken to him lately?" And she's always excited to know that they are doing well. But once, maybe 15 years ago, another friend of mine had sent me a pic of their daughter. I was with my mother when the pic came through my phone. My friend was always an attractive woman, so we were excited to see her baby. But when I checked the photo, I was so shocked that I fumbled my phone. I exclaimed, "OH MY FUCKING GOD!" Until then, I had never cursed around my Christian mother, but even if she had slapped me, I wouldn't have felt it. I had already been assaulted by the sight of Deadpool's estranged love child.

My mother said, "Watch your mouth, boy. Don't use that language around here." Then I showed her the picture. Her reaction was, "Oh!" She took the phone from me and held it in her hand, far away from her face, as if the baby were actually in her presence. She then pulled down her glasses, not to get a better look but to buy time to figure out something nice to say. When that didn't work, she flipped the picture upside down several times as if she was looking at it incorrectly. She finally admitted, "That baby looks like it was hit by the back of a garbage truck." I said it more plainly, "That's an ugly baby." My mother just nodded.

It reminded me of the urban legend of Jian Feng. As reported by many news outlets back in 2012 and 2013, Feng was a man in China who divorced and sued his wife because their children were born ugly (Li, 2013). The story goes that Feng married his wife because she was such a beautiful woman, and he was confident that the two of them could pass their genes on and make beautiful babies. Feng failed to have attractive children with his wife three times and couldn't figure out why his kids looked like little monsters. So Feng investigated his spouse and discovered that she wasn't the natural beauty he thought she was. She had had cosmetic surgery to become all that a man like Feng would want. Angered that he had never consented to having children with a Gremlin, Feng sued and won the equivalent of $120,000 USD (Li, 2013).

That story circulated around the internet for years. I even posted it to my Facebook wall. It turned out to be a favorite, yet false story, according to Snopes. But that still didn't keep two of my buddies from investigating their wives. One of them found out about a bankruptcy his wife filed before they met and had never told him about, but that debt wasn't due to plastic surgery. He was initially happy to know that she was naturally fine, but then he had to face the fact that she had only married him for his money, and that his son's ugliness was all his fault.

Chapter 15
Reason #501
Kids Don't Come with Instruction Manuals

There is something about taking a diaper off a boy that makes him piss in your face. Maybe it's the fresh air hitting his penis that triggers it, or maybe he knows one day you're gonna yell at him for not doing his homework, and this is his way of striking first. Either way, there is no manual on how to avoid having a urine-soaked upper lip. It's as if there is some kind of training camp for boys in the womb on how to fire that thing, but no parent training camp to prepare you for all that parenthood has in store.

From the moment you and your partner get pregnant, you have to make decisions that you have never made before. What to name your child, where to live, whether or not you should tell him who the real father is or whether you should fake your own death so she and the baby can't find you like my buddy Allan after he impregnated a local while on vacation in the Dominican Republic. How do you prepare? Do you stretch? Do you run laps around the track? You are about to embark on a marathon. Do you get a coach? Surely other parents will offer you advice, but no two scenarios are the same. Your friend Kay had a boy. You have a girl. Your parents raised you in the 1980s and you're having kids in the 2020s. Your friend David and his wife were free-range parents, but they raised their kids in Hasbrouck Heights, NJ, and you live in Camden. It's the same state, except Hasbrouck Heights is one of the safest cities in America. In Camden, the playgrounds double as shooting ranges. To put it plainly, you can take other people's advice, but results may vary.

So, where do you learn how to parent? Dr. Spock wrote a book that sold 50 million copies about parenting in 1946 (Gunderman, 2019). One of the things he advocated was babies sleeping on their stomachs. It was later found out that thousands of children were dying of SIDS largely because stomach sleeping is a major contributor to SIDS. Dr. Spock himself died at 94. Guess how he was found? You guessed it, lying on his stomach. It seemed reasonable to follow the advice of a man named Spock. After all, he was a space traveler. But it turned out that his advice helped take out more people than Dr. Kevorkian, another doctor with a funny name who helped solve problems.

My buddy Ben's dad read that book and was so upset that he used the book to spank his kids. It wouldn't have been so bad, except that his dad had the hardcover edition. When he wasn't using it for spankings, he used it to prop up a leg on the kitchen table. When he reached for it during dinner, the kids didn't know if he was adjusting the table or if they were about to feel the wrath of 42 Chapters.

A friend's dad used to spank his children regularly just because he figured they had done something wrong and thought they had gotten away with it. He called it the "Just in Case Spanking." My friends got so used to being spanked that they used to spank each other as some form of training camp for the real thing. They were like kid Navy Seals. They even taught other kids in school how to take a hit and flop on the floor like NBA players do. A lot of people would disagree with my friend's parents' disciplining measures. Organizations like the American Academy of Pediatrics strongly associate spanking with increased aggression in children and teach children that the bigger, stronger person gets their way (Gabbat, 2018). But I assure you that spanking had no long-lasting psychological effects on my two buddies. Both grew up to live in nice neighborhoods and are working as police officers in the hood.

In his book, Dr. Spock advised women to trust their instincts. He must not have had access to social media to see how poor people's instincts were. Before the Coronavirus pandemic, we faced threats from disease. Just like with Covid, people believed that if you caught the chickenpox virus, you were forever immune. Poor parental instincts lead to things like "Chickenpox Parties," where people brought their own children over to play with an infected child so they would get it and develop immunity. Entire neighborhoods would bring their children over. It doesn't take a rocket scientist to know that this was stupid, but it does take a virologist to explain why.

It turns out that, like its cousins HSV1 and HSV2, the virus lays dormant in your system after you get chickenpox and turns into shingles (Carroll, 2019). Now some of those kids who rocked out at that chickenpox jamboree are walking around having outbreaks every time they get stressed. That's what happened to my friend Jessica. Her mom thought she was doing the right thing by intentionally infecting her with chickenpox when she was seven. Now, the stress of her kids causes her to break out and look like the evil villain in a superhero movie. I'm talkin' a DC movie too. Not even the Snyder cut can save her. She just has to tough it out. Her four kids know that stress triggers her painful shingles bouts. Sometimes the oldest two threaten to make her angry if she doesn't do what they want. It's as if she's Bruce Banner, and they know how to bring the Hulk out of her. And when she does get angry, they hide her Acyclovir to keep her in perpetual pain. The youngest daughter doesn't participate in their treasonous acts. She simply hides every time the mommy monster appears. I told her she should've never let that kid see "I Am Legend," but she and Ben never listen to me because I'm not a parent.

My parents simply followed the traditions of their culture. That's what most people do. They look at what their parents did, tweak it and run off instincts. But most people's cultures have no playbook for when a child has special needs. Sure, they have special tonics, concoctions, and prayers for when a kid has a tummy ache, but there seems to be no plan for when there is a stigma associated with a child's condition. I've seen parents ignore signs of developmental delays because they don't want to admit something is different about their child. Who suffers in that scenario? The child, who could be missing out on critical services that can help them early on.

The next step is often regret or even blame. Parents go from the "why me" stage to the "it's my fault" stage. Don't blame yourself if you think your drunken night out with a stranger was the cause of your child's twenty-six toes. Those extra sixteen toes might've been due to your drunken nights out *after* you discovered you were pregnant. There was a manual warning you about that. There were websites, commercials, and warning labels on the beer, and your friends told you not to do it too. Which brings me to my point. Even when some people know the risks, they still don't heed advice. And in the end, who does it hurt? The child who never goes barefoot.

I was fortunate to teach a class of special education kids. I was skeptical at first, but it didn't take long before I fell in love with these children. I had no idea how to work with them, but I had a great paraprofessional who knew the kids and knew exactly what to do. The experience was different from regular education. There was a lot of repetition from day to day and week to week just to move the needle an inch. It took patience, and the results achieved educationally were far less than what you could expect from children who didn't have their challenges. Education is a science. We have methods already developed and continue to tweak them. And if the science experiment blows up, it won't be in our faces. Instead, it's like the exploding battery pack in a Tesla. It only affects the driver and passenger. Parents have to drive home and deal with the long-term care of the kids and all that comes with that, while Elon just shrugs and trolls more people on Twitter.

As an educator, I was just a small part of my kids' day. I wasn't their parent. I usually didn't have to deal with their medical emergencies. One of my former colleagues and friend worked with a non-verbal tenth-grade boy with severe and profound disabilities who seemed to be having a medical emergency in class. The boy was groaning in pain. My friend followed all the procedures according to the school, attending to the boy and notified the boy's mother of the incident. The mother, who was single-parenting her autistic son, reported to the teacher that the boy had been doing the same thing at home while grabbing his crotch. My teacher friend advised her to take him to the doctor. As a mother to a son, she had no idea how severe the condition could be but was afraid to take action. The next day it happened again.

The school notified her a second time, and she was forced to come to the school to pick him up early. Recognizing that she couldn't delay this any further, she took the son to the doctor. According to the story I was told, the doctor diagnosed the boy with epididymal hypertension and was told that because the boy didn't know how to relieve the tension himself, the mother had to "open the valves," so to speak, to let some of the steam out.

At sixteen, I told my girlfriend I suffered from the same condition, but back then, we just called it blue balls. Despite all my groaning in pain, I was forced to knock the edge off myself or suffer in silence. But in this kid's case, his mother, who once had to duck from being hit by her son's piss every time she changed him, now found herself having to duck from being hit by her son's jizz.

I wouldn't have wanted my mother jacking my johnson in tenth grade. She might've thought I was Mr. Fantastic based on how much it had stretched since she last bathed me as a toddler. My mother thankfully relinquished my personal hygiene duties to me at four years old, but for that mother, well, Dr. Spock didn't have a chapter on that issue.

Life gives you spoiled milk. What are you supposed to do with that? Some people figure out their own cheese recipes, and others throw it away. I'm not a cheese maker. I'm not a chickenpox partier, either. I like to write but only when inspired. I don't write my story on the way to the emergency room. Parents have to write their own manual as situations arise. For some, that's the beauty of being a parent. For others, that's the burden. You can probably guess which of the two it would've been for me. If you can't, read the next chapter. You'll figure it out.

Chapter 16
Reason #928
I Swore I'd Never Do Math Homework Again

I see parents work 10-hour days, spend 2 hours in their cars or public transport and come home to cook dinner and do homework. Three of those things are unavoidable, but the fourth is perfectly preventable. These parents aren't trying to get a higher degree or learn a new skill. They are doing their children's homework. And let's be honest, a lot of them aren't just helping. I know because I've seen it first-hand. Some teacher decides to do his or her job and give their students work that actually helps them learn, and Junior really doesn't want to do it. I say Junior because it's usually the boys who get the most frustrated and give up. I know that because I was one of those boys.

Mom or dad is looking over their kid's shoulder for the few free hours they have left in their evening, trying to encourage their lil "genius" along. This kid thinks this should come easy or "forget about it." But the work doesn't come easy. It wasn't meant to. And once it gets difficult, he gives up. If you're a parent, you already know where this story is going. If you're not, well, keep reading. This is your future every Monday through Friday after work. After the student gets frustrated, the parent tries, to no avail, to get their kid back on track. This becomes frustrating to the parent, who hasn't done this kind of thing for two decades or more. This results in confusion for the parent, who realizes that they are teaching this stuff totally differently nowadays. So the parent asks the student more about how they taught this. Without fail, there is some level of anger directed toward the school for changing the way things are taught. It's usually math, btw. So the parent asks the kid again, "Did your teacher explain this to you?" The teacher spent the whole day on this for the past two weeks, but the kid needs an easy out, so he says, "No. He never taught this." But the teacher isn't the one at the kitchen table with his head in his arm playing with his pencil. So the parent has to face the reality of the situation. It's 8:30 at night. The kid has given up. Yelling won't work, although they give it a try. Eventually, they simply give their wayward student the best answers they can to fill out in their handwriting. After all, you can't let the school know who really does the homework.

I am determined that this will never be me. When I graduated college, it was the end of an academic career plagued with frustrating after-class work fatigue. I had always done well in school where I was able to discuss the topic freely with my professors and other students, but once I got home, I shut down. I dreaded homework and throughout my academic life, missed a lot of homework assignments.

As a freshman in college, I majored in journalism and was an excellent journalistic writer. I loved the news and was told by the professor, Mr. Patterson, that I was the best writer in the class. But when I turned in my articles, almost always late, they came back marked with C's and almost never included constructive criticism. I asked Mr. Patterson about this, to which he responded, "Your articles are great, but they are always turned in two or three days late. News happens fast, so either you hand in your homework when it's due, or I advise you to change your major." The very next day, I went and changed my major. I would've done it that day, but it was late.

I had struggled with homework from an early age. I'm uber familiar with the nightly scenario between parents and kids because my mother and I wrestled with each other at the kitchen table for years. My mother taught me to read before I started school, and I was not a willing participant. Then when school began at five years old and structure was introduced into the mix, things just got worse. I was traumatized by my first-grade teacher Mrs. Harrison. Mrs. Harrison was an incredible educator, but she seemed to forget that this was first grade, not the first year of grad school. Mrs. Harrison was the Danny Rand of the classroom. She ruled with an iron fist, and no one dared to cross her. And she taught our class with a marathon runner's endurance from the moment the first bell rang 'til the sound of the last one at three o'clock. I half suspected she reported to a second job as a corrections officer at Rikers, but if she did, God help those fellas in "the bing."

Mrs. Harrison didn't end the days with a simple "goodbye." She didn't just give us one assignment and say, "See you tomorrow." No, she loaded us down with more homework than most kids got all month. And I'm talking about the kids in high school. Every day she wrote out on the chalkboard at least 15 different homework assignments to be completed by the next day. She filled the chalkboard from one end of the 20-foot wall to the other. We had to copy whatever she wrote on the board into a separate book that was designated to store each night's tasks. She gave so many assignments that the school wouldn't allow her to use the copy machine.

My dad loved the fact that Mrs. Harrison challenged us. My mother? Maybe in theory, but she was the one tasked with helping me get through it. My struggles with homework didn't end there. It continued through high school. In 7th grade, I failed my first class: math. All the homework help in the world wouldn't have saved me. I just didn't get it. I ended up having to repeat that class in 8th grade. My mother, recognizing my struggles, helped me through the second round. And she's also credited with helping to prevent me from repeating other classes, although not all.

My mother and I now joke about one memorable evening when I was in tenth grade. I was supposed to read a chapter for a test the next day in literature class. I was behind in that class, and she didn't want me to fail, but I wasn't putting in any effort to prevent it from happening. It was 10 o'clock at night when my mother found me in the bed, nearly passed out. She decided to read the chapter aloud to me. I still struggled to stay awake. My father witnessed my mother reading to me as I crept off into slumber-world and was appalled. Apparently, he had never heard of sleep learning before. Later in life, I would utilize this technique to learn Spanish. While I may "Hablo Espanol" now, as a result, I still failed that literature test.

My dad owned his own business, went to school, and taught GED classes several nights a week. His job was to get me out the door to school in the morning. My mother worked long days like many parents do. She cooked and took care of the house and struggled with me on homework. As hard as they both had it, there are single parents out there who are doing both jobs. They get the kids to school in the morning and still have to pick them up, cook, take care of the house and have to read an entire chapter to their tenth grader so they won't flunk out. These are parents who probably thought they would have a partner to help share in these responsibilities. At least in my home, my parents were a team.

Nowadays, there are more single-family homes than ever (Kramer, 2019). Sure, as a parent, you can Google your way out of tough questions, but there is still the added pressure of doing it all yourself. Not to mention understanding what Google just explained to you. Back in the day, education was fractured. You had teachers who, like Mrs. Harrison, went above and beyond to exercise the minds of their students. Then you had teachers who just didn't care and everything in between. This resulted in Americans not all knowing the same things and some even believing that the Earth is flat. So the U.S. looked around and realized that places like China didn't teach flat earth theory. They taught their kids in a standardized way. Ignoring the fact that our cultures are very different, the Department of Education decided to implement a standard that all students would complete and test for (Lee, 2014). This birthed the "Common Core" standard, a system of educating students that would grow to be hated by teachers, students, *and* parents.

I applaud them for trying. In a global competition for the best talent, the United States couldn't afford to fall behind. They had to do something. But Common Core was met with vitriol. Parents complained that the national standard introduced homework that they couldn't assist their children in completing, especially math homework. Parents weren't used to the new, convoluted process of adding, subtracting, and *arithmeticking*. It wasn't good enough to simply give the answers on paper anymore. You had to show how you got there. Parents were pissed. Before Common Core, if students were to show how they got their homework answers, they would have had to bring a picture of their parents from the night before doing it for them. Maybe my mom could've come to school and read for the entire class.

Despite all my mother's hard work, I had reached a point where I didn't want to go to school at all. I was discouraged. It was frustrating for me and my parents. They struggled to find a solution to my educational woes. I ended up in summer school multiple summers at Stuyvesant High School. It was the only school in the city that my school would accept credit for. One summer when I was there for math, I had to talk two students out of killing the teacher. Five years before Columbine, these troublemaking students who I was sitting next to in the back of the class interrupted a lecture by the teacher, who promptly admonished them. One student, Kamal, got upset and whispered, "I should smoke this motherfucker." I didn't know if he meant apologizing by offering the teacher a blunt or killing him. I figured it out quickly enough when he opened his backpack and showed me a two five. I played it cool and asked him what kind of gun it was before the other boy also brandished one in his book bag. I told them to "Chill. He's not worth it," and asked them to see the guns later. They both zipped up their bookbags and stayed quiet for the rest of the class. That was some quick thinking on my feet. If only I could've done math that fast, I wouldn't have been in that situation, to begin with.

I never wanted to see geometry or algebra again. I don't care how long it will take two trains, heading toward each other at 120 kph each from a distance of 400 miles to collide. I'm not "carrying the one" anymore. That's what Alexa and Google Assistant are for. The truth is, after all the work my mother put in at the table with me on math homework, I never use any of it. The basic stuff Mrs. Harrison taught us in first grade still serves me well, though. Addition, subtraction, multiplication, and division are all I have ever needed. I'm not an architect or an engineer. I'm a voiceover talent. I read to other people through a microphone. Most of us only struggle with math when we need to figure out the tip. Just download a tip calculator and keep it moving.

These experiences helped shape the way I view homework. I had done so much homework in Mrs. Harrison's class I figured that from then on through college, I didn't need to do anymore. Then the experience of flunking math in high school and having to take summer school almost killed me, quite possibly literally. Realizing how much it was all for nothing turned me off. By the time I graduated college, I pledged that I would never do it again. I would never do homework another day in my life. Not mine. Not anyone else's either.

Chapter 17
Reason #809
The Mom and Dad Bod

This is the part of the book where I have to Mansplain a few things. It may make some people uncomfortable. I have to talk about what children do to our bodies. No, I'm not talking about your four-year-old climbing all over you and accidentally stepping on your nuts. Nor am I talking about the 80-pound eight-year-old who still wants you to pick her up, which hurts your back. I'm talking about how parents neglect their appearance and allow their self-esteem to diminish instead of attempting to maintain those qualities that attracted their partner to begin with. I'm talking about both men and women while acknowledging that women in our society bear the brunt of this scrutiny. It's brutal. I know, but here it is.

I've never swiped right because I saw a woman who looked like she had a great personality. That would be absurd. If you believe anyone does, then you probably believe that people used to buy Playboy for the articles. They didn't. I've also met several women whom I've dated long-term in public spaces, like the mall, the airport, or in a nightclub, and in none of those cases have I thought about how great their conversations may have been. I introduced myself because I found those women physically attractive.

I think I speak for most men and many women in this respect. We men are very visual creatures. Evolution has made us chase after the qualities in women that pop out the most. We like breasts, thighs, buttocks, and hips. It may all sound like something you'd order from the KFC menu, but these are the things that signal "sex" to our brains and subconsciously suggest this woman is a strong candidate to make a baby with. It's not just men who are attracted by physical attributes. Broad shoulders, physical strength, confident demeanor, and height are often markers of a man that attract women to him. But while women may factor in other qualities, including some superficial ones like apparent wealth, men take the cake when it comes to superficiality.

Men want young and hot-looking women, and when we get what we want, we don't want that to change. But it *does* change once children are involved. When a couple gets pregnant, the number one priority is the baby, and neglect of oneself is almost immediate. The father stops going to the gym, and the mother... well, I wouldn't advise her to keep going hard like she used to. Change occurs in her body. Hormones are racing all over the place. Body parts are swelling, and not just the ones dad was looking at that landed them in this predicament in the first place. I'm talking about faces, arms, and ankles. No one gets turned on by swollen ankles.

And then there is the belly. Okay, I admit it. There is something sexy about the pregnant belly to me, especially the ones that stick straight out. But while I strangely admire how that bump pokes out, as opposed to what I used to love in a flat belly, I can't help but think, "Damn. That looks like it hurts." Men would never do something like that to themselves. Men wouldn't let someone else do that to them. If men were able to get pregnant, we'd want to shoot the person who got us into this situation. After all, they shot in us, and showed no mercy. In fact, the culprit is probably a mass shooter and should be taken out. Now we're stuck like this for nine whole months? In New York, where I'm from, nine months is the time you could spend in jail before trial for possessing an illegal firearm (Orlando, 2012). So why would I throw myself in prison? Yet some women consider this time that includes morning sickness, frequent urination, mood changes, and more, to be one of the most joyous times of their lives. And this is all before the main event.

No amount of epidural could make a man push a whole person out of our bodies. No amount of money or cocaine could convince us, either. And where would it come out of? But women are troopers. I've seen a video of a woman giving birth where she was pushing as hard as she could and the father passed out. She was doing all the painful work, and all he could think about was how he will never be able to brag about the size of his manhood to her after an entire person came out of her vagina. After he saw how much pain she could take, it became apparent to him that it really wasn't "all his," and he succumbed to syncope. Meanwhile, she's grunting, crying, and shitting on herself, trying to introduce their bundle of joy into the world. The dad couldn't have taken the actual pain. He would've died, and not just because childbirth carries a real risk of actual death (about 295,000 worldwide per year) (World Health Organization, 2019). But women do it anyway. They put their bodies through it because, instinctually, it seems worth it.

Once the baby is born, the woman goes into full mommy-mode. That sexy body becomes a milk factory, producing more lactose than Horizon Organic. This milk secretes at the most inconvenient times, and there is often more than she can handle. I've witnessed a woman leaking milk through her shirt. She was apparently embarrassed, but I understood and expressed empathy for what she was going through. When I was 19, I used to ooze through my clothes a lot too, but only while I was asleep. This happened to this lady every day, and she had to keep a pump with her to help mitigate what was happening to her body. Although, thinking back on it, maybe I should've had one too.

Women experience weight gain, stretch marks, saggy tummies and breasts, and even changes to their vaginas. On average, 47% of women gain more than the recommended weight as it relates to their BMI, with some women gaining as much as 62 pounds (*Centers for Disease Control*, 2015). For high-income earners, a personal trainer, a tummy tuck, breast lift, and vaginal rejuvenation can be the answer. For most women though, financial resources usually go toward Pampers and care for their new baby.

It's not just the saggy breasts and leaky milk, either. The mind is a part of your body too. According to CDC, as many as 1 in 8 women in the U.S. suffer from postpartum depression, a number that is as high as 1 in 5 in some states (CDC, 2020). Women can experience feelings of anger, isolation, loss of energy, hopelessness, doubt, and even suicidal thoughts or thoughts of harming their children. For some, these feelings never go away, and it's hard to predict who will be affected. Relationships become affected by both the psychological and physical effects of childbearing. After the physical changes, a lot of people are psychologically drawn to something or someone else (Dickson., 2019). Whereas you swiped right to get her, now you're swiping left to push her off the bed. The changes in appearance can be dramatic.

Back in college, I remember a few women who used to excite me every time I saw them. Without fail, whenever they would walk by on campus, I would eye stalk them like a desperate weirdo. They were my perfect type, the same type I still have 20 years later. And while my taste in women hasn't changed, the women I used to want to taste have.

At the start of my junior year in college, I met this girl, Tee, who I tried to hook up with. She was a freshman. When I saw her for the first time, I almost passed out. I tried speaking to her once to get her phone number, but she shot me down. It was embarrassing the way she did it. She looked at me like I was trash. The eye she gave me was the "I would NEVER talk to you" eye. Over time, I befriended friends of hers, who all put in a word of recommendation for me. But after one spoke to her on my behalf, the friend came back to me and advised me to give up trying. I gave up trying, but I never gave up hope.

Men can keep a woman in mind for years, sometimes decades. We plot how to impress her the next time we see her. My plan was simple: "Dane, if you see her again, just be an older, more mature version of yourself. Don't be so anxious or eager. Play it cool." So, years later, I played it cool when I saw her at homecoming. I hadn't been back to my alma mater in years. Lots had changed at my school. But the friendships I had remained strong. Many of my friends only communicated with me through phone or social media, but we picked back up right where we left off as if we had never missed a beat. That included her friends, who were still my friends.

I was in the minority of the group. I wasn't married or divorced, and I was child-free. Listening to all the stories about my friends' lives made me curious. "Hey, where's Tee?" "Oh, she's coming. She just has to get her kids ready," I was told. "Kids? Wow! Tee has kids too?" I was a bit disappointed but still excited to see her. Turned out she had two kids, but the father was not in her life anymore. The new, more mature me might have had a chance at that hook-up. Plus, now I had evidence that she liked it bareback. Even more reason to give this another shot.

Tee arrived with her kids. I heard her before I saw her because there was a big ruckus when she arrived. All the other friends swarmed her and her kids to greet them. When I turned around though, I couldn't find Tee. A woman was there, but the Tee that I knew wasn't. I mean, she was, but she wasn't. Tee was like two Tees. Shocked by her physical transformation, I just stood there stunned. Tee rushed over to me with her arms wide open as if she realized that not hooking up with me back in college was a mistake. Tee used to be sexy. Now I was faced with having to hug her on the installment plan. I was polite about it, but the air was let out of my balloon, and not just because she hugged me so tightly. I couldn't believe what I had witnessed. It was the greatest collapse since the Falcons blew an enormous halftime lead in Super Bowl 51. How did this happen? I took one look over her shoulder and answered my own question: "Oh, them damn kids."

Tee had become comfortable. Over time, dealing with grown-up responsibilities, her body didn't seem to matter to her anymore. Adulting has a way of reprioritizing things. I was doing way less adulting, so I was still consumed with the same things that occupied my mind when I was a junior classman. Back in those days, I was skinny too. I was so skinny that holding a pencil felt like I was hoisting a rocket launcher onto my shoulder. I hated it. I used to wear nice baggy clothes to distract from my underweight physique. I remember hooking up with a girl who kept stopping me mid-action to complain that my bones were hurting her. It wasn't until after college when I started lifting weights with my friend Dolvett, that I started bulking up. I had hoped that women would look at me differently, and they did, but life had moved on.

I discovered that women aren't the only ones who lose it. A lot of men think it's okay to let themselves go. Women's criteria for choosing and keeping a mate tends to be less physical. Yes, women do pick men using visual cues like height, muscles, a nice smile and hair, but women more often are on the lookout for confidence, intelligence, and persuasiveness. Subconsciously men know this. We know that what we say to women is more important than what we look like. That knowledge translates into us doing all that we can to maintain and grow our pocket size, all while ignoring the fact that our belt size is growing with it.

As long as we are providers, that's all that seems to matter to our partners and to us. Society has told us that that's our role, and so we fulfill our duty at the expense of our physical health and mental wellbeing. Men are far less likely to seek out a doctor for physical ailments or emotional woes. We're either conditioned to believe or born into thinking that if we provide food for our families and a few additional luxuries, it doesn't matter if our eyes fall out. Our daughters will still love us, and our wives will still accept us.

All this is not to say men are completely unconcerned with our bodies. A man will still pose in the mirror, remembering the days when he still "had it" and feel excitement when he sees just a fraction of it peek its head out. It's that moment when he gets one of the six stomach muscles to poke out from the fat that he thinks "Yeah!" and mentally high-fives himself. For just that one second, he harkens back to his glory days of fun parties and one-night stands with random women, before he's interrupted by his 4-year-old walking in on him asking, "Daddy, what are you doing?"

You know how bodybuilders shave all their body hair at bodybuilding competitions to accentuate their muscles? Well, dad bodders do the opposite. They grow endless forests of hair on their chests and back to hide their dwindling muscle definition. Some even wear a gold chain to decorate it. There were a lot of bald guys at homecoming, and each year, they got balder and balder. That's natural and understandable, but I was tempted to ask them, "How many months are you?" and "Have you picked a name yet?" Some of them only needed a red suit and a long white beard to work the mall during the Christmas season. How many six-packs did they have to drown themselves in before their six-pack disappeared? A lot. They had totally fallen apart.

They became apathetic. It's as if they had done everything they could to get the woman of their dreams, then awoke to the nightmare of fatherhood and honey-do lists. Before children, they were basking in the glow of each other's love and attention. He was still excited when she commented on how strong he was and giddy when she rubbed on his arms. These days, she just rubs on his belly.

My buddy Ben is like that. He doesn't recognize how he's changed. We used to meet up at the gym and lift weights together. He was Schwarzenegger strong without steroids or the shrunken penis. He was naturally muscular. But after his first kid, his priorities changed. Those big arms turned into jelly, probably as a result of eating so much of it with his daughter. And that six-pack was replaced by an impenetrable mound. Ben never got the point that he wasn't the same guy as before. He kept trying to fit into his old designer shirts. The Armani shirt he had when he met his wife was missing a button that his belly had forcibly popped off. It was so embarrassing for his family that his wife had to hide the shirt from him. When he realized it was missing, she denied knowing its whereabouts and then proceeded to "help him find it." It was quite funny. They were like two kids running around the house playing hide and seek with a shirt that she had stashed in her car trunk in a box labeled "Goodwill."

All the while, I was in the gym, getting stronger and fitter. At one time I considered doing fitness shows but decided I didn't want to shave my chest hair. Women still rubbed my arms, and my six-pack hadn't been co-opted by Coors or Miller. But my workout partners cycled in and out. The ones who showed up were childless, the guys whose children were grown, the ones who never saw their children, and the married guys with girlfriends. Sometimes their lives changed, and I wouldn't see them in the gym anymore. They would either have children, have to babysit their grandchildren, be in court fighting to see their children, or their wives would find out about the side chick. Either way, their life changes meant that throughout the years, I could never maintain a steady gym buddy.

Having children shifts your priorities... and if those priorities include focused care for your body and looks, be prepared for a shocker. My body matters to me. Since I was very young, I worried about my health. And like many young people, I obsessed over body image. When I finally realized that I could change my body, I did. I could never be tall, dark, and handsome, but at least I could be chiseled, dark, and handsome. Okay, maybe just chiseled and dark. After I achieved my fitness goals, all I had to do was maintain them. Old age and testosterone loss will eventually take their toll, but I'm not just gonna throw in the towel. I'm gonna fight. It's important to me, and it's hard for someone like myself, who doesn't have distractions and responsibilities, to understand how it's not important to others who also used to prioritize the same things. I don't want to change. The dad bod is a real threat, and I'm too afraid of becoming Bob from accounting.

Chapter 18
Reason #315
I Can't Always Protect Them

I was 11 years old. I had been a latchkey kid since I could remember. My parents were small business owners, PTA members, second job workers, and for many years, advanced degree pursuers. They did all they could to make life better for themselves and their children. But I spent a lot of time alone. A lot of kids in the neighborhood were like me. The police would come to our school and teach us what to do in the event of danger. My parents amply prepared me for what to do and what not to do when I got home. I knew how to cook and heat up my meals and was conditioned to keep an eye on the stove when I used it. I locked the doors. I listened for any unusual noises. I even kept a baseball bat nearby in case the house was home-invaded. Growing up in New York at that time, there was danger everywhere. And because my parents couldn't protect me at all times, I was responsible for protecting myself. But I admit, I was always scared.

I walked home alone from school every day, went straight into my house, and locked the door. Like clockwork, it was the same seamless routine of traveling one block and turning the corner to reach my elementary school. Short of occasionally stepping in dog poop, there had never been a problem. But life is funny like that. You have to be ready for it to rewrite the script. And one day, while I was in the 5th grade, it did just that.

I was walking down the street toward home, and sitting in a car parked directly in front of my house was a strange man. He had watched me walk down the street. I reached the sidewalk near my home. Window rolled down, he continued to gaze intently at me. I felt threatened, so I walked past my house, never even looking at it. As I passed by, he yelled, "Hey, how old are you?" I didn't answer. Recognizing that this guy might have been the neighborhood Woody Allen, I picked up my pace. He exited the car and from about 25 yards away yelled again "Hey! How old are you?" "I'm Eleven," I yelled as I hauled ass out of there and went to my closest relative's house.

My life might've been a lot different had I tried to go into my house. If not for what I learned from home and school, I would've been the victim of his twisted ventriloquist act, where I would've been the puppet. Luckily, I was prepped for these scenarios. My parents didn't raise no dummy.

For my entire childhood, I lived in fear. I was often without the physical protection of my parents. But honestly, there are just so many things that even they couldn't protect me from. I grew up near the end of the cold war. We had bunkers in school basements. I feared being nuked like my mother's leftover Sunday dinners. But when the iron curtain went down, my guard didn't. Terrorists, school shooters, white supremacists, building bombers, and Mayor Giuliani were still on the loose. This was real life. And these threats loomed outside any shield my parents were capable of providing.

There was another incident that occurred when I was 16. Older and bigger, I had learned to identify and avoid danger a lot better. One summer evening, I was heading home from my girlfriend's house when I spotted three suspicious guys eyeing me in a similar manner as the pervert had when I was 11. I attempted to employ the same avoidance tactic, but these guys made a U-turn in the middle of the street to follow me before jumping out of their car to surround me. They started yelling at me, and one put his hand in my pockets. They cornered me near a fence, and when I asked who they were and what they wanted, one of the thugs grabbed me by my neck, pushed me against the fence, and choked me. What could I do? All of them had guns. When the ordeal was over, I ran home and told my parents what had happened.

We went to the precinct the next day to report these gangsters. My dad was on the community board and had frequently collaborated with the police. The officer asked if I knew who did it, so I gave him the badge number of the thug who choked me. It was Officer Ken Campbell, a member of an undercover unit that terrorized children in the neighborhood. The incident was sent to the Civilian Complaint Review Board and investigated. Two years later, they contacted me with their recommendations: the cop was to receive sensitivity training. Officer Campbell got a slap on the wrist. I got an unprovoked choke to the neck.

My parents couldn't protect me against police assault or any kind of assault. There were so many moments in my life when I needed and wanted to be protected, but my parents were nowhere to be found. It wasn't their fault, but at the same time, it was. When they decided to have me, they signed up for the job of parent and guardian. I know now that it was impossible to face the dangers with me every time, but coming up in the world, that's exactly what I expected. That's not realistic. But try explaining realism to a toddler, a tike, or even a teen. It's a hard concept to teach.

Protecting children from harm doesn't just come in the form of guarding their bodies. It's just as important to guard their minds. Psychological damage can happen without an officer ever choking your children. One of the biggest threats to a child's well-being is right there in their pockets. Social media allows basically anyone to have access to your kid, and for your child to participate in their own destruction. Social media gives predators and bullies an avenue to interact with your child where they can be touched even while you are sitting next to them.

In 2010, Rutgers freshman Tyler Clementi killed himself by jumping off of the George Washington Bridge in New York. He had been cyberbullied by his roommate Dharun Ravi and another student who had secretly filmed Clementi kissing another man in his room (Pilkington, 2017). While his parents knew, Tyler had kept his sexuality a secret from most of his family and friends. It was a different time then, when Tyler's private same-sex interactions could easily be exploited. Ravi posted the video on Twitter and promoted it to other students like some kind of main event. He then threatened to post more videos of Tyler's personal encounters.

Tyler's not the only one. Hate and harassment online are commonplace. I've spoken to female and African American gamers who have been bullied online and constantly called racist and sexist names. When talking to a young African American teen about it, he said, "After a while, you just get numb to it." Players can report these bullies to the gaming platform, but I suspect the offenders won't even get sensitivity training.

Young people face other threats, too. In October 2021, Frances Haugen, a former Facebook employee turned whistleblower, testified in front of congress regarding the company's reckless disregard for and profiteering from teens on their platforms (Feiner, 2021). Haugen's job was to study algorithms that helped get users hooked to the platform so they would spend more hours viewing ads. She found that the company, now Meta, knowingly baited teen girls who were most vulnerable to the mental harm caused by Instagram photos, which promotes unrealistic body images. Teen girls' self-esteem was being destroyed, resulting in eating disorders, depression, and even suicidal thoughts (Paul & Milmo, 2021).

The easy solution would be to keep young people off of social media, but the pressure to be on these platforms is so great that teens may be prone to conceal their online involvement from their parents (Palmer, 2012). You can warn them about the dangers, but that's like warning people how much closer to diabetes and coronary artery disease they are before they eat that belly-busting burger and super-sized freedom fries. The cheeseburger doesn't fall far from the tree. Kids don't always listen.

We've all heard the saying, "What doesn't kill you makes you tougher." Well, I never exactly wanted to die to figure out how tough I could become. I could've lived without some of my experiences. But it's true in some ways, too. Baby Boomers are tough as nails and lived through some of the hardest stuff. Yet, they're still pansies compared to the greatest generation who lived through World Wars One and Two. But when I look at younger Millennials and certainly almost all Gen Z's, I see people who wouldn't survive a mugging by an ice cream scoop on a hot day.

So is the answer to protect at all costs? To hover over children, bearing the brunt of all their stress as many Baby Boomer and Gen X parents decided to do with their kids? When I ponder that, I consider a quote attributed to the late Dubai Sheikh Rashid bin Saeed Al Maktoum, "Hard times create strong men, strong men create easy times. Easy times create weak men, weak men create difficult times. Many will not understand it, but you have to raise warriors, not parasites" (Rathore, 2021). I don't want to be a parasite, Mr. Sheikh. I just want my mommy.

I guess that's why some parents directly expose their kids to danger. It's kind of like herd immunity. Sure, your kid might die in the process, but if they survive, they'll only have to worry about the psychiatry bills when they get older. Cruel experiments aside, this is the approach taken by the anti-helicopter moms and dads known as "free range parents" (Rebecca, 2016). Back in my day, they were just called "Parents." I can just see the looks on the faces of my mother and father when they find out that they were ahead of their time, except my parents, and parents for millennia before them, were free range parents out of necessity. Free range today is now a parenting movement.

Perhaps the one mom who most exemplifies the free-range movement is Lenore Skenazy. Back in 2008, she let her 9-year-old ride the New York City subway by himself. Skenazy left her son Izzy in midtown shopping and was like, "Yo peace! I'm out. See you at the crib," and gave the boy, who navigated the subway home without incident, a MetroCard and directions home (Bloomgarden-Smoke, 2015). The woman, who was a New York Sun Columnist, wrote about it in her column. She was instantly vilified by the public for her "reckless" parenting and called every name in the book by everyone who hadn't been crushed by the financial crisis that year and who still had time to quote books. People were truly outraged. They had forgotten about the days when parents, out of necessity, had to teach their kids independence, critical thinking, and life navigation skills. The public had awarded Skenazy the title of world's worst mother. No one knew the name of the person who came in 9th place for participation, but more than likely, it was someone whose helicopter parents told them they could be whatever they wanted to be in life.

I find it hard to understand where the line is between the harm caused by the stress of having to protect myself versus the harm caused by helicopter parenting. Life happens. And it doesn't give a shit about you. The Ken Campbells will choke, and the child predators will stalk. The only solution is to avoid life itself.

Chapter 19
Reason #806
I Don't Need to Leave a Legacy

The legacy argument is both the most ubiquitous and worst idea people use when pushing the narrative that we all must have children. It's predicated on the idea that we all share the same values, and simply put, we don't. The 2020s are quite different from the 1820s when exercising your options was not an option. We're able to research topics like life satisfaction among parents just by pulling out our phones. We know more about the threats to our planet than we did before. We are not stone-aged people. We don't have to think like them.

The legacy argument goes like this: Who's gonna carry on your legacy? Who is gonna take care of you when you get old? And what if your parents had thought like you? The legacy argument tries every trick in the book to convince people that they are wrong for not carrying on their last name (Greer, 2022). It attempts to reduce a person's humanity to a single accomplishment, one that is not much of an achievement at all.

Who is gonna carry on my legacy? No one, and that's okay. Humans, because of narcissism, believe that when they die, they still have a presence on earth and that they are eternally monitoring their legacy with pride. The problem is that even if this is true, we have no control over what happens to our legacy. We may hope that our legacy is like Joe Jonas or Joe Montana, but instead, it could be more like Joe Jackson or 'Joey' Stalin. I hope that my legacy will be something I actually accomplished, like having worked with children in the public school system and helping to educate and inspire thousands. Or like having written a children's book, *Dana the Procrastinator*, with the goal of teaching kids the value of time. I've traveled the globe to learn first-hand about the plight of other people, and I give back. I donate to causes that help people. Each day I look to do more. These things are my legacy.

People often claim their children as their legacy because, for many, that's all they have. Judge me for my works, not because I can ejaculate in a woman. I would rather be remembered for the performance I put on the nights I potentially made the kids than for making the kids themselves. Having sex and getting pregnant shouldn't be the gold standard for accomplishment. Literally, most people on earth can do that.

If having children is your biggest achievement, then where does it end? Do my kids have to leave a legacy too? At some point, I'll be forgotten. My legacy will be quickly upstaged by my children's legacy. That will likely be within two generations. Here's a good example. Name your great-grandmother's father. Get my point? Who is Albert Einstein's dad? Name his children. You likely don't know the names of either, which means that if Albert Einstein was remembered for his legacy of creating children, he would've already been forgotten, and if his dad was to be remembered for his legacy of creating Albert, his name too has been overshadowed by his son's works. Instead, we remember Albert Einstein for the theory of general relativity. That's his true legacy. His contribution to science and in turn humanity will be forever tied to that.

My grandfather produced more than 20 children and only financially and emotionally supported a few of them. Is my grandfather an accomplished guy because he made so many kids? Based on the legacy theory, with that many kids, he should have a statue erected somewhere in his name. But when he died, he was buried in a modest grave that eventually no one will visit. He neither has a statue nor any other erections to add to his "legacy."

The second part of the legacy argument is that if you don't have children, you will die with no one to take care of you. I have thought about this a lot. It hits home for me because, of course, I don't want to go into old age without human connections. I think about my grandmother who passed away in 2017. She had nine children and struggled to raise them alone after my grandfather abandoned her to create more children with other women. She sewed clothes and did odd jobs for years while doing her best to raise her seven sons and two daughters. My grandmother was born in Cuba. When she had an opportunity to come to the United States, she did, and one by one, she filed for all of her children to come to America. Those children went on to have their own lives and families, with only two exceptions.

My grandmother went to college when she came to the States and, at 50, got her nursing degree. But when she got ill just a few years later, she had to cut her career short and needed to be cared for herself. Of her nine children, just one, who didn't have a family of his own, took direct care of her. My uncle sacrificed his own life and dedicated it to my grandmother until she passed away at 96. My uncle is an incredible man for what he did, but now at seventy-plus years old, he's gonna need to work fast to have nine kids of his own in hopes of having someone to take care of him.

My uncle is a rare breed. They don't make them like him anymore. Ask any nursing home worker. As few as 10 percent of nursing home residents get regular visits from family members. And as for financial support, it turns out that in the United States, families are mostly not helping seniors (Gaugler, 2005). Seniors in the US rely on a mix of their families, government assistance, and money they, themselves have saved. People who earn more likely contribute more to aging family members, but people who earn less aren't as capable. In America, seniors are largely left to pull themselves up by their walkers. In fact, they often have to contribute to helping their children make a way in life (Petersen, 2021).

So who am I gonna rely on? I'm gonna rely on the same people that a lot of other people rely on, even when they have children. I'm gonna rely on the same person my grandmother would've relied on had none of her nine children stepped up and sacrificed their lives for her. I'm gonna rely on the same person that my uncle will rely on. I'm gonna rely on myself and build connections with others to have a rewarding life for as long as I can. When it comes time to check into a nursing home, I will have saved up enough to pay for one and trained long enough in Jiu Jitsu to defend myself against the attending nurses.

What about carrying on my family name? What about if I have daughters who marry and take their husbands' names? The people who argue this point generally don't put much thought into the argument. They also don't know that my grandfather had more children than the Saudi Royal family and that he was one of 16 children. My last name will take hundreds of years to disappear.

Here is another popular argument: "If your mother thought like you do, then you wouldn't be here." My mother was 21 when she had my older brother and waited until she was 28 to give birth to me. Women can have at least one child a year, but my selfish mother didn't have those seven kids she could've had in between my brother and me. Those poor kids aren't here. According to some people's logic, the kids that were never conceived are suffering because they never had a chance at life. If my mother thought then the way I do now, I wouldn't know the difference.

What legacy are we leaving? We have less than 50 years before some old dictator who's got five minutes of breath left says, "Hey, I wonder what this red button does?" With just one press, he'll reduce the population from seven billion to seven hundred of the dumbest people the planet has ever seen. Thanos was right. We humans have a lot of problems. We have a global freshwater shortage, rising sea levels, food shortages, and we are depleting our oceans of fish (Chowdhury et al., 2017). That's just the tip of the melting iceberg. The y chromosome is disappearing. Men have less sperm than their grandfathers. Women in their 20s are less fertile than their grandmothers were at 35, and the suspected culprits are chemicals like pesticides, and phthalates found in plastic (Brehm & Flaws, 2019). This is the legacy we're leaving. It's one where we take and don't give back.

Even if humans manage to get our act together, scientists hypothesize that the earth will be consumed by the sun in 5 billion years anyway (Tomaswick, 2021). What will there be to remember? Who will be here to be remembered, and who will be doing the remembering? Our sun will become a red giant and consume the planet (Powell, 2017). We'll be sucked into the sun like poor people were sucked into Sou Sou in 2020. And just like how all our money disappeared, our planet will be gone. Even if you believe in one of the three major Abrahamic religions, you believe that the world will end. The world is like one giant game of musical chairs, except we keep adding players and removing more and more chairs. Eventually, we will be stuck with billions of players with nowhere to sit. We are destroying our planet.

Chapter 20
Reason #6
Kids Have Cooties

I worked with kids in the public school setting for six years, and they were the sickest six years of my life. I was a twenty-something-year-old guy. I lifted weights and ran almost every day. I ate a healthy diet and never engaged in bad habits like drinking and smoking. I was extremely fit. But no amount of fitness could prepare me for the Petri dish that is elementary school. It was terrible. Every year I would enter the school year healthy, then be knocked down by colds and flu every six to eight weeks. Some of those days, I came into work feeling spritely, but by lunchtime, those kids had infected me with their cooties and I'd start looking over my shoulder for the reaper.

The first few years of working with kids, my immune system took a major hit. I had to start getting vaccinated for the flu to avoid missing workdays and feeling miserable. Still, those little suckers got me. If it wasn't the flu, it was a cold. One year the kids gave me diabetes. I don't know how that happened, but I suspect one of them sneezed on a cupcake I had for lunch, and tadow, I was stuck sticking my finger for the next decade. That's why I avoid eating around kids. A kid will sit at a table next to you, cough over your food, and act like nothing ever happened. Meanwhile, you're stuck having to decide whether to eat that meal or throw it away. Long before Covid, I stayed six feet from anyone under 18 whenever possible. I avoided my friends' kids' birthday parties just to avoid the birthday cake. I don't want to eat after they blow their cooties all over it. The only way I'd eat a slice was if the kid used a box fan to blow out the candles.

Kids have no decorum. They cough without covering their mouths. They wipe their snot with their shirts and, even worse, their hands. Then they touch things without washing their hands. They sneeze everywhere. They just don't care. And it doesn't matter how many times you correct them on it, they just repeat the behavior and say "sorry" if they think you're upset by it. They roll around on the ground and eat things off the floor. They spread their cooties on the playground and then bring them home to their parents. They bring home colds, flu, lice, ringworm, and now hepatitis and Covid. I'm convinced Covid was started by kids in Wuhan, China, who were playing with bats in their basement. Then one was bitten. Not one of the kids. One of the bats. That bat then flew away and dripped blood everywhere, including an innocent meat market, where it just spread from there. I usually don't believe in conspiracy theories, but that one seems plausible to me.

I know parents who got Covid from their kids multiple times. The parents were one gasp of air away from calling the ambulance while their kids, who made them sick, were unfazed. Ben and Jessica told their kids countless times to keep their masks on in school and daycare, but their kids still gave them Covid. Twice. Ben was stuck in the bed feeling like crap, and they were running around the house playing with toys and demanding that he buy them Taco Bell for dinner. Can you imagine having Covid and Taco Bell at the same time? I'm glad he finally had the cojones to tell them "No" for once. Ben would've been running for the border of the toilet bowl. Picture what would've happened whenever he coughed. Regardless, the kids were fine, but he and Jessica were out for the count.

Parents like Ben and Jessica have it tough. Across the country, parents often have to decide between staying home with sick kids and losing out on pay or sending those sick kids to school. In most states, there is no paid leave for parents, and there is no national law that protects their jobs. The United States is not conducive for families. You either work or you lose out on pay, or worse yet, your job (Paid Sick Time, 2018). In the UK, which has ⅕ the population of the U.S., parents lose out on a total of three million working days a year caring for sick children (Jordan, 2021). British families lose on average three working days a year to look after their young ones (Office for National Statistics, 2019). I couldn't find a figure for the US, but I'm sure it's significantly more. America has a much poorer social system. Childcare in the U.S. is difficult to find, and often expensive. So parents send their kids back to the very place that made them sick in the first place: school (Smithers, 2017).

Elementary schools are the worst. Older children can at least take care of themselves for a few hours while parents go to work.

But that doesn't mean that they have any fewer disgusting habits when it comes to being infected. It was college kids who so happily and rapidly gifted the nation with the initially high Covid cases. The same kids who years earlier were spreading Mono around their high school hadn't learned their lesson and were down in Miami spreading SARS 2.

When the pandemic hit, I stayed locked down to avoid potential threats. For many parents, the threat WAS COMING FROM INSIDE THE HOUSE! Massive invisible germ clouds surround children wherever they are. When I stopped working for the school system, I also stopped getting frequent colds and flu. I stopped getting flu shots and haven't had the flu since. I've even been able to stop taking my diabetes medicine. Now that should tell you something about those cooties carrying kids.

Chapter 21
Reason #1
They Cost Too Damn Much

They cost WHAT? WHAAAAAAAAAAAAT? ARE YOU INSANE? The cost of raising a middle-class child in the U.S. from birth to 18, as of 2022, is between $286000 and $476000, according to the U.S. Dept. of Agriculture (Bradford, 2010). At first, I thought those figures were erroneous, but I checked other sources and confirmed the numbers. And the Dept. of Agriculture would know. They count how much we have to feed these kids. At one time in history, having children paid off. Kids used to work the farms starting at six years old, doing backbreaking manual labor that no American presently wants to do. But those freakin' child labor laws changed that for everyone, and now we must rely on mules to recruit seasonal farm workers from Central America. These lazy kids want back pay for the work they used to do on the farms and they aren't ashamed to put their sweaty little palms out to collect.

Everybody wants in on the baby manufacturing business. Immediately after a baby is taken out of the baby oven, the baker wants his cut. In 2018 in the State of Florida, it cost a family on average $22,015 to deliver a baby (Learish, 2020). You gotta make a lot of bread to afford that. You could buy a crooked governor and still have money left over for a senator's vote for that kind of dough. We regular people don't have that kind of money, nor the support of our legislators to make things easier for families.

Most people never realize the true cost of children. They just do what they have to do to make it work. The day-to-day costs add up so quickly that people only worry about how far today's dollar will stretch, ignoring that they could probably retire in Mexico for what Billy and Tommy cost them over time. They kick the can down the road when it comes to expenses like college, hoping that the kids will get a scholarship, a loan, or simply figure it out for themselves. The costs of food, healthcare, and emergency medical expenses, clothing, transportation, activities, and even the cost of having a place to live with one extra bedroom all balloon the price of raising your bundle of joy (Laponsie, 2021). Those expenses are immediate and take precedence. My dad used to joke about having to pay for the extra room that I grew up in. He'd laugh and say that he and my mother weren't "just my parents;" they were my "pay-rents." Now that I'm an adult and have to pay rent, I get it, but that doesn't mean I have to "parent" too.

Now I understand why parents used to let their kids sleep over at Michael Jackson's house. They needed someone to sue to help cover the cost of raising them. Parents are slipping and falling in front of moving cars just to pay for their kids' college. I was talking to a friend about the cost of sending his daughter to Southern University.

I would tell you what it cost, but by the time you Google it for yourself, it will have likely doubled. The cost of college in the U.S. makes parents feel like they're trying to purchase *bread* in Venezuela. *Bread* may be expensive in Venezuela, but college there only costs $80 a semester (All About the Students, 2021). In the U.S., *bread* is cheaper, but college is $80,000 a year (Hess, 2019). No "*Wonder*" we hate them. Plus, U.S. students have to buy books, pay for room and board, on-campus meals, and transportation costs (Bouchrika, 2021). All of this for a general science degree.

My parents raised me on 176 dollars a year. I had one pair of sneakers that were too big at the beginning of the year but fit just right by year's end. The way my mother predicted how much my feet would grow made me think she was Nostradamus. I didn't have Jordans because I didn't need Jordans. I needed a nice pair of sneakers, some decent jeans, and a tee shirt. My parents were smart. They knew I would only wear clothes for a few months before my next growth spurt. Even today, I keep it simple. I value-shop. I go out looking nice in an outfit I bought from Target for thirty-seven dollars. Once in a while, I spent forty-seven, but I'm not going much higher than that. My parents taught me to act my wage.

Growing up, that wage was zero, and I acted accordingly. Other kids had a higher wage, and they acted accordingly, too. I knew better than to act like them. I remember when I was in high school, the boys used to play stop motion football in the schoolyard. The schoolyard was all cement, so stop motion was a way of preventing a player with the ball from advancing toward the goal line without tackling them to the hard ground, but by no means was it a gentle sport. There were several kids, like my classmate Mike M., who were really good at running the ball in stop motion football. No matter how hard defenders tried to stop Mike M., he was determined to score. And he wasn't afraid to sacrifice his clothes to get a touchdown.

I decided to stop playing with those boys when I saw Mike M. with a completely ripped shirt from a recent stop motion football game. He could afford to rip his shirt. He had a role in the movie *Home Alone* and starred in commercials. I vacuumed the living room in my house for five dollars a week. My mother wouldn't have been cool with a ripped shirt. I would've had to wear that shirt for the rest of the school year and all summer vacation long until we went school shopping for the next year.

My parents weren't just gonna brush things off and get me a new shirt. We had limited resources. Nowadays, kids think money is unlimited. Every time I go out with Ben, and he has one of his kids with him, they always want him to buy them something. Usually, it's food, but sometimes it's a toy or a game. We can go someplace totally unrelated to food, toys, or games, and they still have food, toys, or games on their minds. Ben's kids were at a funeral and interrupted the eulogy to ask when this is all gonna be over 'cause they want daddy to buy them a toy pony. It didn't matter that it was their grandfather's funeral. They just wanted to hurry up and bury him so they could stop by Walmart and Pizza Hut. They always want to spend Ben's money on something.

My generation had to eat before we left the house. We could've been going out to eat at a restaurant and we still had to eat at home first. I guess that was to make sure we didn't run up the tab at the all you can eat restaurant. Can't a kid enjoy his only restaurant outing for the year? After all, it's my birthday! But no! My generation's parents also made sure we used the bathroom before we left the house. I know finding a bathroom in public for a kid can be challenging, but I also think they didn't want us having to stop at Walmart or McDonald's and get any ideas.

That's a major difference between generations. Our parents were building a future for us, so they were frugal-minded. Nowadays, parents like my friend Ben are suckers. He falls for the bathroom at Mcdonald's trick every time. I told him he needs to tell his kids "We're not gonna fall for a banana in the tailpipe," and make it sound natural. Those stops usually cost him sixty dollars or more. His girls can really throw down some food. When his dad died, Ben was driving the lead car in the funeral procession and led 40 cars through the McDonald's drive-through. The kids claimed that they were saddened by the loss of grandpa and needed a happy meal, and Ben acquiesced. Consequently, it cost all the parents in the cars behind him money, too, as each one of their children decided they were hungry and depressed at that moment. Some of those kids never even met Ben's dad. Well, at least Ben's dad got to spend a few extra hours above ground.

It's not just the food bill that's higher when you have kids. Everything costs more. They leave the lights on when they exit the room for hours. Then when they turn into teens, they run up the water bill by staying in the shower for 45 minutes. And what for? They should just masturbate in their room instead of running up the water bill to $1300 a month.

I've never been one who could ignore the cost of things. For most of my life, I have been financially insecure. My awareness of how spending money today only amplifies my woes. Tomorrow is ever present in my mind. I've been criticized for what I spend on my mental health vacations, but in total, I haven't even spent $286,000.

I never thought I would earn enough, so I had to make hard decisions to maximize my quality and enjoyment in life. I had ambitions but never believed that pulling myself up my bootstraps would lead to a financially enriched life. I, like so many people, resigned myself to temporary pleasures and taking solace in what I could achieve, as opposed to what I couldn't. And that made me happy. I reached for the low-hanging fruit, then came up with dozens of innovative ways to prepare and eat it. I've had my highs, and I've had lots more lows. I've been burdened with debt, to the point that not long after college, I was bankrupt. I couldn't keep up with my bills. I had tried to enrich myself by purchasing an investment property with a business partner. Instead, he scammed me, and I was left holding the bag. I lost my job working for the school system mostly because of illness. Eye-watering medical bills have piled up over the years and then the 2008 financial crisis hit. It was a gut punch.

Success was something that I had only seen in other people. I thought I deserved it. I always believed that I was too intelligent to be poor, so I did what any smart person would do. I made a plan. The plan was to suffer short-term to achieve a long-term goal of happiness. The plan was to use what I had to get what I wanted. The plan was not to allow any person to hold me back financially.

And the last part of the plan was to eliminate anything from my life that would financially weigh me down. If I didn't need it, then I wouldn't have it. In all of this planning, I realized that children were a "don't need," a "weighing me down," *and* a "person to hold me back financially."

A lot of things came to mind when I thought about the high costs of raising children. I don't do drugs, but I could blow through a lot of blow for what it cost to raise just one. At $286,000, kids cost as much as the median home price in America at the time of this writing. You have to go through credit checks and jump through every hoop an underwriter can think of to get the keys to a house. Yet to embark on the major financial responsibility of having a child, you and a cosigner of the opposite sex only need to pull down your Underoos.

I have dated a lot of women, and have always tried to remain friends with my exes. But whether or not I have been successful in remaining close with them, I've never maintained financial ties with them after breaking up. Sure, I have had a mountain of credit card debt from excessively traveling with one of my exes, but I've never owned a house with a woman, had a woman owe me money or vice versa, or left a relationship where either one of us had to pay the other anything. This has reduced the stress of breaking up. I have never had to weigh the monetary costs of exiting a relationship with the mental toll of staying in it. Sadly, that calculation is one that millions of people face.

Being a parent is tough. Plus it comes with a cost. Benjamin Franklin said, "In this world, nothing can be said to be certain but death and taxes" For nearly $300,000, I'd like to know what my money gets me before I invest. I want to be sure that working a job that I might not like, long nights at the table helping my child do homework, and stress over childcare will result in something I can quantify. But that's not how it works. Kids are a risky investment. I may spend $300,000 to raise them, and they still may not be willing to travel 300 miles to see me in the nursing home.

Chapter 22
Reason #620
When My Relationships End, I Want a Clean Break

I remember being at a mansion party around 2008 where I was standing by myself, holding up a wall. A guy who seemed like he knew as few people there as I did walked over to me and started making small talk. He asked me who I knew there and what I did for a living. You know, the normal stuff. So I asked him the same, and he told me he was a dentist. The conversation quickly devolved from there. He went on a rant about his ex-wife and all the child support he had to pay her. He said she was sucking him dry, and he hardly seemed to have a boner over it. He had a bone to pick, and he told me all about it. He hated this woman, and from how he described it, she was dragging him through hell. The stress of dealing with his ex was so great that he needed to talk to me, a stranger, because the money he would've spent on a therapist was going toward child support. I thought about this guy the day I had my vasectomy. He and lots of guys like him were the reason I subsequently updated my Facebook status to "Marked Safe from Baby Mama Drama."

I have heard too many real-life tales of the struggles of dealing with an ex-partner. When two people are bonded by children, they can be held hostage by a relationship that they no longer want. Both women and men have told me stories of their ex-partners using their mutual children as pawns. They use the court system as leverage over the other party to settle disputes that often arise due to issues that existed during their relationship or as a result of their break-up. I'm a guy. When I hear these stories, unsurprisingly, I mostly identify with men because if I had ever had a child with a woman, that's the side of the courtroom I would be standing on. The male side.

The men I have known caught in child custody and support issues are mostly good men who love their children. They weren't sperm donors; they were men who supported their children financially and emotionally. But the list of men I know who have been boxed out from fair access to their children is long. I have one friend whose son's mother wouldn't allow him to see his son even though she was receiving support. She moved more than 1000 miles from where they ended their relationship. When she left Georgia with his son, I suggested that he call Liam Neeson because this seemed like a scene from *Taken*. Liam's "special set of skills" surely could get his son back. My friend dismissed that idea and opted to go about things through legal channels.

Several times after driving to see his son, the mother denied him the right to do so. Their personal relationship impeded his relationship with his child, so he gave up. He went back home and attempted to keep phone contact with his son, but for years she even denied him that access. A funny thing happened over those years. He worked on developing himself in every aspect of his life, including his finances, and became a prosperous businessman. Hearing of his success, the child's mother reached out to him. He paid her years' worth of back child support, and at 14, the son decided to move in with his father. He never looked back. Someone once asked my friend why he didn't fight harder to be in his son's life. I would've responded, "Why don't you ask his mother why should I have to?"

What could he have done differently? Men report that the court isn't much of a solution for them (Aminu, 2017). One of my male friends told me a story of needing to file some paperwork with the court regarding a case he faced against his daughter's mother. He called the court clerk on the phone and asked about the procedure for filing the paperwork. The clerk told him that they were unable to give him information on how to file and that he would have to seek advice from a lawyer or consult the law library for legal guidance. He had his wife call the same courthouse and speak to the same clerk to ask the same question. Not only did the same clerk explain to her in detail how to file the paperwork, but the clerk also went on to send my friend's wife the paperwork in the mail with a self-addressed, stamped envelope so that she could return it to the court for free.

Another male friend of mine who has two children wanted primary custody of his boys when they were younger. He hardly fit the stereotype of a deadbeat dad. He loved his sons and wanted to be there for them every day. He and his ex-girlfriend were about equal when it came to financial stability. That is to say, neither had much money. But my friend did what he could to benefit his sons. He hired a lawyer to aid in his fight. But the lawyer bluntly said, "Unless she is strung out on drugs, you have no chance of winning this case." He was right. My friend didn't win the case. He won the right to see his sons once every other weekend and the right to pay child support. He was a weekend dad every other weekend. And let's be honest, being a weekend dad is like being a glorified babysitter. Still, he loved his boys and any time with them was valuable. This guy decided to pay more than the court required of him. Over the years, he did all that he could for his boys. He was there as much as possible, every two weekends, spoiling his boys, but it wasn't enough. His sons always seemed broken. Their mother was both mentally abusive and neglectful. When his oldest son became a young man himself, he blamed my friend for not doing more to get him away from his abusive mother. They have an estranged relationship to this day.

One of my male friends calls me the smartest guy he knows because I don't have children. He spent $75,000 in lawyer and court fees fighting with his child's mother. The only thing he got was the right to pay $800 a month in child support which he says he has on autopay. That's $172,000 until his child is 18 years of age. Add that to the $75,000 he spent in court, and he's short a lot of bitcoin. If he had invested that money in the S&P, he would've had… I don't know. I'm no financial advisor, but I know he would've had a lot of money.

The worst thing for him and so many guys like him, is that the child's mother gets to control the narrative. She told their child some pretty horrible things about him. Mothers are usually awarded primary custody by default, and she, like so many, used that as a vehicle to score points against my buddy. Their relationship might have soured, but they should've worked cooperatively to raise their child. They don't. Instead, the child has shown disrespect for him as a result of messages fed to him by the mother. As long as I've known this guy, he's been nothing but decent. I've spent time around his new wife and her kids, and he's an upstanding man. He seems to have taken the path of least resistance by simply paying his $800 monthly and avoiding the drama.

Then there is Joe. Joe was the cousin of one of my best friends from college. At the end of his senior year in HS, he got a classmate pregnant, and they both agreed that they didn't want to be teen parents. He was going away to college, and so was she. Together they made the hard decision to have an abortion. Joe gave his half, left for school, and he lost touch with his high school fling.

Joe is a good guy. He did well in college, and graduated, and got a decent job. He lived the bachelor life, thinking he had learned his lesson. That was until he turned 31. That's when Joe got a call from his former fling. This was a hookup call. She wanted to hook him up with his 12-year-old son. She never had the abortion that they agreed on, and was now demanding years' worth of back child support. Joe was hit harder than Stacey Morgan was by that Walmart truck. He didn't know what to do.

But did I mention that Joe was a good guy? He truly was. Although angered by the fact that he was lied to, he embraced his responsibility. When he told me, I couldn't help but think about 12 years of back child support. Where was he *gonna* find that kind of money? Joe was the first guy I ever knew in Atlanta to purchase both a gun and a motorcycle, and I couldn't help but pray for every gas station owner within 30 miles. But he wasn't that kind of guy.

Joe's story came to exemplify the risk involved with sex. It was one of those rare horror stories that I would eventually find out weren't so rare. As I got older, I had to learn to balance the risks involved with my favorite hobby and the reward in the comfort that it gave me. But Joe's experience wasn't the only reason I decided to have a vasectomy. Over the years, I had my own scares. I watched other friends have their own children accidentally and on purpose. I watched their children motivate them to be successful or drive them to depression. But truthfully, I had witnessed many more miles traveled in those proverbial vehicles of gloom and regret than I had seen happiness.

So why did I go on a rant about this? Because the idea of feeling powerless scares me. The sense of being all alone with the chips stacked against me in a court system that is supposed to protect my rights scares me. Paying $800 a month into another household while I struggle to put a roof over my head scares me. I can't imagine paying that much money and having a child who's been led to believe I'm a bad father. I could be blowing that kind of cash in a strip club instead. When my buddy goes to pick up his kid, the kid acts like he doesn't love his own father. At least if I try to pick up a stripper, she always acts like she loves me. For a couple extra dollars, I can even get her to call me Daddy.

I tell these horror stories not to attack women, which I'm sure some of you think I'm doing, but to support my argument about not wanting children. As a man, I have to consider the actions of the opposite sex that would affect my life. But I also know the horrors that women experience. I have ample numbers of female friends who are held captive by their dirtbag children's fathers. Just like not all women are angels, not all men are stand-up guys either. Female friends tell me things about their children's fathers that make me want to show up on the dude's front porch with a lead pipe and a team of angry pro-life protesters. But then I remember, "Oh, who am I kidding? Pro-lifers don't care about mothers or babies after birth. I'd have to show up with gang members from MS-13." Either way, it's upsetting some of the things that men do to their baby mamas.

Women have to make tough decisions, often before they even reach the point of splitting with their children's father. Some endure physical and psychological abuse. Many women have to decide whether to stay with a cheating partner for the sake of their children or to leave for the sake of their sanity (Dworkin-McDaniel, 2017). The ones who choose to leave can face a bumpy road ahead. The ones who choose to stay contend with dodging STDs like Neo dodged bullets. These are tough choices. Leaving means potentially abandoning a stable home, financial security, and partnership that helps lighten the heavy load of child raising. But the conditions driving them to leave take them down dark, unpredictable roads that could dead end in an alley where a meth dealer named Steve offers to buy their daughters for twenty bucks.

When women decide to leave, the obstacles don't end with the end of the relationship. Women are stuck to the same cheating, abusive, or irresponsible guy they had that child with. Marissa Alexander was trying to leave her estranged, abusive husband, Rico Gray, when he threatened to kill her. After the Florida woman barricaded herself in a bathroom, Gray busted down the door and shoved her to the ground. Marissa escaped to the garage where she retrieved a gun. When Gray, who had a history of abuse against women, made threats against her once more, she fired a warning shot into the wall. Marissa Alexander was arrested and initially sentenced to 20 years in jail despite invoking Florida's controversial Stand Your Ground law. The sentence was eventually reduced, but the mom, who had just given birth nine days before the incident, paid with three years of her life in jail (Amber, 2020).

Many of the problems between fathers and mothers stem from money (Hutson, 2007). There are a lot of men who don't want to pay at all. Some of those same guys also post pictures of their latest trips to Cartagena, their Nike collections, or make bold claims about how well they're doing. They buy their kids expensive outfits, take pictures of them for 'the Gram,' and boast about their children. But when these guys show up in court, they tell the judge that they're broke. I knew a guy who had his own business where he made six figures. When the child's mother asked for an increase in child support, he hired an accountant to fix his books to make it look like his company only paid him eight hundred dollars a month. When they went to court, the judge saw what he earned and reduced his child support payments to almost nothing. Sure, he stuck it to his son's mother, but he also stuck it to his son.

That kid's gotta eat. A growing boy can devour Ronald McDonald himself and still have room to eat Dave Thomas *and* his daughter Wendy. When I was a teenager, between my raging hormones and random growth spurts, I ate a lot of Wendys too. I opened our refrigerator so often that the heat in our house used to kick on. That would've been another bill for my mother to handle on her own had she ever had to decide to leave my dad. And bills would've been just one aspect. My mother would've been charged with the task of raising a boy in New York, managing my behavior and anger issues, and educating me on her own, all while staring into the face of a child whose image reminded her of the man she was forced to leave. Too many mothers have to make that choice. I consider myself lucky that mine did not.

Being stuck with someone you hate just because y'all have a kid together is probably like a rat being stuck to one of those yellow sticky mouse traps. And to think, just like when they were making the baby, women must pretend to like it for the sake of the kid. I asked a friend, who is a mother, what it was like escaping her daughters' father.

At the age of 16, I met my daughters' father. At first, he was a gentleman. He swept me off my feet, spent money on me, bought me roses, and took me out to eat. That was a big deal at 16. Before I knew it, we were spending all of our time together.

At age 18, I got pregnant with my first daughter. That's when things started to change. He was making a lot of illegally sourced money, and it started getting to his head. Women started climbing in his bed, and everything I said got on his last nerves. He was cheating and became physically abusive. The first time he hit me was over a simple disagreement about me going out to enjoy myself. He slapped me so hard that I lost hearing in my ear. More than 20 years later, I still have problems with my left ear. I hid the abuse from my family. I was young and I thought I had my child's best interest in mind.

At just 20 years old, I had daughter number two. I absolutely love my daughters, but if I could rewind time, I wouldn't have had any children by HIM at all. If I had known about abortions, I probably wouldn't have had a second child because I was fed up by that time. I just didn't know how to escape. Things got so crazy and abusive that I began to fight back. I even tried to kill him twice. I once poured bleach into his macaroni and cheese, thinking that it would take him out. The second time I shot at him. I remember the exact moment that I gave up. I sat on my bed and I prayed to God to remove him from my life. He was so toxic, and I was so weak. I saved up about $5000 and planned an escape to Florida, where my oldest sister lived.

The best thing that I could do was decide to leave. At 22, I was scared and feeling alone. All I knew was that I couldn't allow my kids to grow up in such a toxic environment. I couldn't allow them to see their father break me. I didn't know what was on the other side, but I knew it had to be better than where I was, so I got on a bus with three boxes and headed south. I never looked back, not for a second, not even for a phone call to argue or ask for closure. All I did was move forward with the best decision of my life. Since then, I promised myself never to allow anyone to have that power over me again.

She made one of the hardest decisions of her life. She chose to protect herself and her children. But it couldn't have been an easy choice. Whenever you have children with someone, you're bonded to that person, and that bond can take you to dark places. My friend's experiences aren't my experiences. Her experiences aren't even most women's experiences. But it's still something that happens to a lot of women.

Listening to these stories has taught me one thing: When a relationship is over, and I am no longer stuck on you, I don't want to have to be stuck to you.

Chapter 23
Reason #730
Anthony Bourdain

Anthony Bourdain was a guy I admired. I don't look up to celebrities just because they're famous. There has to be something special about them, and Anthony embodied that uniqueness. He was a New Yorker like I am. He was a world traveler who embraced all cultures like I do. He started from the bottom and stayed there most of his life like I have. He was an introvert like me. I admired and regarded him as a beacon of hope. He didn't get his big break in life until he was in his forties and had failed repeatedly at soliciting published writing opportunities. And most of all, his last name has the word Dain in it. What's not to like except for the spelling?

But the thing that struck me most about Anthony was that he had a dark secret: his struggle with depression. He battled dark demons. Regrets, fears, self-doubt, and pain all haunted him even as he did television shows, filmed documentaries, wrote books, traveled, and even broke bread with a president. The voices in his head told him that this life wasn't worth living even though his, at least from the outside looking in, was one of the most admired lives on earth.

These were the same voices that told Robin Williams that this [life] wasn't funny anymore. After all that Anthony had accomplished, he hanged himself inside a French hotel.

Life is hard, and for so many people, it's filled with pain, regret, fear, and doubt. I suffered with it for most of my life. I have dealt with sleepless nights marred by anxiety attacks. Don't worry. You don't have to call me to talk me off the ledge. Over the years, as I have accomplished many of my personal goals, I have carved out satisfaction in my life. But I haven't forgotten how challenging it can be just staying alive. I've gone from a guy who, at 14, wanted to run out into traffic and get struck by a Park Avenue cab to someone who won't oversleep because it feels too much like death. I am glad to still be here, but having been given the option, I would've let that other sperm beat me to the egg.

When we look at celebrities, we think they have it all. What are they worried about? But life itself is a problem for millions, maybe billions of people (Emmott, 2021). Too often, our understanding is limited to what we can see and feel. We lack empathy and understanding of things and people we don't see. Life, for a lot of people, is hell. Getting up every day and having to face yourself, your demons, and your responsibilities is taxing for so many and if it's not for you, you may simply be in denial.

So how do kids play into this? Anthony was born on June 25, 1956. On June 28, 2018, just three days after his 62nd birthday, he decided he had had enough. This journey through life wasn't what he chose. It chose him. His mother, Gladys, and his father, Pierre Bourdain, chose him. They chose him because they had the hope that all parents have. The hope that their children will live a life of joy, love, success, adventure, fun, freedom, longevity, and good health. In a 2014 episode of "Parts Unknown," Bourdain described his childhood as being filled with love and attention. He self-reported that he was happy growing up. How could his parents have known that one day their son would be a famous chef and television star and still not believe the life they gave him was worth living?

It's a far-out concept for people to grasp. We didn't ask to be here. We were brought here by ambitious parents who themselves thought life was the greatest gift they could give a person. Or they decided that perhaps their children could live out their dreams for them. Or maybe Anthony's parents normalized giving life, like most people do, and never considered what Anthony would be. They never considered that he might be, above all things, unhappy.

How many people are like Anthony Bourdain? According to the American Foundation for Suicide Prevention (AFSP), on average, 130 Americans kill themselves each day. That's 47,450 American deaths by suicide per year (American Foundation for Suicide Prevention, 2022). That's a lot of Americans who don't think life is worth living every year. In 2020, nearly 70% of them were white males, and 52% of all suicides were committed with firearms (AFSP, 2022). I had the unfortunate luck of witnessing a man kill himself when I was 17. One day I was on the subway in Brooklyn, on my way home from school, when I saw a man leap in front of an MTA 4 train. He was standing just feet from me when he took that leap of non-faith. I remember the loud thud the moment the train struck and dragged him underneath it. Hours later, when I returned to the station, I watched the clean-up and saw workers shoveling his body parts into red trash bags.

When I was younger, I identified with that man. I identified with Anthony. I didn't want to be here either. Early in life, I would question the meaning of existence, why I was here, and who put me on this earth. I questioned everything. At 4 years old, my older brother explained to me that God brought me here. I clearly recall thinking that God was cruel for doing so. My nighttime ritual seemed especially torturous. Each time I was tucked into bed, I was reminded that I might not live to see the morning. "While I lay me down to sleep, I pray the lord my soul to keep. If I shall die before I wake, I pray to God my soul to take." What a horrible thing to teach a kid! That prayer was, in part, why I've always feared falling asleep.

To me, life was feeling a sense of perpetual powerlessness, and I hated it. Everyone around me controlled my fate, from my parents to my older brothers, aunts, uncles, cousins, and any random adult I interacted with. Life meant bowing to their will. No one treated me poorly, but everyone had expectations of me and assigned me responsibilities. Life felt like slavery.

I never grew accustomed to what life expected from me. I have suffered health issues since I can remember. I've had chronic and often debilitating migraines since I was six, yet I was still expected to go to school, concentrate, and perform at a high level. I always had issues with sleep, energy and… I forget what the last thing was.

Oh yeah, memory. Life gave me a deck full of diamonds and told me to play spades. I was unhealthy and unhappy. Once my brothers left the house when I was 7, I was lonely too. I wasn't having fun. Throughout my teens, I suffered from depression. I hit a low when at 14 years old, I called a teen suicide prevention hotline in the middle of the night, and they hung up on me because I was whispering, which violated their policy.

But something happened one day that changed my outlook. I discovered girls. Well, actually, I had always been interested in girls, but they finally discovered me. I drowned myself in sexual pleasure, which evolved into greater self-confidence. That confidence made me more social and gave me friends all around New York. I reached a point where my depression about living life turned into anxiety about losing it.

Several years ago, I was talking to a client who specializes in sales and marketing. He explained to me that in marketing, if you tell potential consumers that they can obtain something for free, they are less inclined to act than if you tell them they may lose something. For example, a person who stands to gain a free watch is less likely to get up and drive to the mall than a person who may have a similar watch taken from them. People have a significantly greater passion for losing than winning. You see this in politics. If you tell people they can get free healthcare, they're not as fired up as the people who are told they could lose their healthcare.

This is what happened to me. I began valuing my life and wanted to see more, do more, and connect more. The same life I once wanted to end became the life I didn't want taken from me. I began suffering from death anxiety. At night I suffered from anxiety attacks and my sleep issues, which existed before, worsened. After I witnessed that man on the subway end his life, I began waking myself up from deep sleep just to make sure that I was still alive. I never wanted fame, but I wanted to live forever. Yet the countdown had already begun. It began the day I was born, but I finally started counting with it.

I have done a lot of fun and exciting stuff since then. My twenties were filled with self-exploration and mindless fun. Then I discovered the world in my thirties. The first time I had a chance to travel out west and see the Pacific Ocean, I reflected on the days that I wanted to take my life, and I thanked God that I didn't. But with all that I have done in life, if I had been asked before I was conceived if I would've wanted to be born, my answer would've been a resounding "No." The idea that I could gain so much and have it taken away was too great of a price to pay. It's not worth it. The worry that I face about what's next is too great, and the powerlessness I have in fighting it is too painful. Unfortunately, I couldn't have prevented it either. Life doesn't come with a consent form.

In 2009 my Uncle Teddy passed away. He fought aggressive lung cancer for several years until he couldn't fight anymore. This uncle, like all of my aunts and uncles, was a hard-working guy. I never heard him complain. He just did what he had to do. He was a cook in the Army for several years. He knew how to kill the bacon, bring it home and cook it. He was always telling jokes. He was a funny character. He was a strong guy too. When cancer came knocking, he saw who it was and slammed the door on it. It kept knocking, but he held that door shut.

When it finally got in the house, he kicked it, punched it, scratched it, and fought it off. My uncle was even put in hospice at one point and refused to let go of life, so they sent him home. It was months later before he was readmitted to hospice, and I saw him for the last time. I was in the room with him, my mother, and his wife. The fighter in him was still trying to fight, but the war was already lost. The man who always kidded around was crying, wishing that someone could save him. That was a powerful moment in my life because I knew the road he was traveling was the same path I would eventually take. If I could've saved him, I would have. But I couldn't. He was in a room with people who loved him, but he was all alone.

No one asks us if we want to be here, and no one can stop us from dying. We comfort ourselves in life by saying things like, "death is part of life," but if we aren't born, we don't have to worry about that particular part. We don't have to worry about the bills, the laws, the job, the kids, or even the worry itself. We would know nothing of this world, and just like when people don't watch the news because they warn you about all the murderers in your neighborhood, ignorance is bliss. Few people understand or connect with my perspective on giving life. We have all been given life and just go about living it. It's normal to us. They sprinkle a few religious texts over it and wash it down with a bit of booze, and it all seems fine. But for the people who experience life through the lens of the Anthony Bourdains of the world, there isn't enough alcohol on the planet to sell them on the idea that life is anything but cruel.

Chapter 24
Reason #911
The Book of Brittany, Part 2

One year after Brittany admitted to cheating on me, we continued our tumultuous relationship. We were two firecrackers who ignited each other's lustful fires, and I couldn't escape her. But things were different. While the lovin' was sweet, the revenge was sweeter. Brittany had cheated several times, and for me, it had grown into both a competition to see who could top the other person and an excuse for me to sew my wild oats while still maintaining our dysfunctional relationship.

Still undressed and lying in bed, Brittany was unusually quiet. Perhaps my man powers rocked her to sleep. As I dressed, ready to leave her dorm room, I looked over and noticed that she was awake. We caught each other's eyes. Mine, satisfied from our evening together, hers filled with tears. Concerned that perhaps I had broken something by being too rough, I asked, "What's wrong?" She replied, "Dane, I love you, but I know that you are never going to marry me."

I didn't respond to her verbally, but I didn't have to. I loved Brittany, but it was understood that this was going nowhere.

I didn't break anything inside of Brittany. It was already broken when I met her. What I was doing was grinding the broken pieces into fine grains of sand. I always wanted to get married, but knew I could never marry her. Her infidelities spun off into multiple infidelities of my own, which like a ball of yarn, could never be rolled precisely back onto its spool. I enjoyed the attention of other women. I enjoyed having a woman fly me across the country to go skiing, only to return home to Brittany, who greeted me with open legs. I enjoyed the days in bed with Karla and the nights I spent in Brittany's dorm room.

Karla was a girl who went to my school. I had finished all my credits and was working a job at the UPS Store while I waited for graduation. Karla, like Brittany, had two more years until graduation. In my senior year, she and I became great friends and then hookup buddies. She was a great cook and invited me over all the time to eat her amazing southern-style cooking. Dessert was always served in the bedroom and was always the best part of the dinner. Brittany would sometimes call during meals, but Karla never minded licking the plate while I paused to talk to my girlfriend. When the calls were over, we would usually laugh about Brittany not picking up on what was going on and then would continue feeding off one another.

Brittany and I had learned at least one lesson from the year prior. After our pregnancy scare, we made the mutual decision that she would start taking birth control pills. Despite her shortcomings in many areas, she was responsible for taking the pill nightly. She never missed a pill. By April, 2001, she had been taking it for about eight months. We weren't willing to repeat what happened the summer before. I remembered that scare all too vividly. I thought about it every time I was intimately involved with any woman, including Karla. Karla and I had it covered. We had grown close, but not too close. Brittany was the only woman I shared that kind of intimate contact with. I had it all figured out.

Brittany and her family decided to take a vacation to Africa that month. I would miss her but also knew I would have ten days of uninterrupted fun with Karla. She was excited too. Brittany that is. She prepped for the trip, packing all that she needed and getting all of the required inoculations. To send her off, Brittany and I had one more sexual encounter the night before she departed. I figured that if I couldn't go to Africa with her, I would send my soldiers in my place. We passionately thrusted up against each other's bodies until we both climaxed. She came first. I came last. Then she left. Only once before had I felt like this when we were done. My spidey senses were going off. I didn't tell her, but I knew then that not only were my soldiers escorting her to Africa, but they would also escort her back.

I worried the entire time she was in Africa. Brittany came back to Atlanta. I tried not to stress her about the subject, but I mentioned that I was worried. She was in disbelief. After all, we had taken precautions. After more than a month, she decided to ease my fears and took a pregnancy test. Instead, the test confirmed my fears. She was pregnant. The girl I knew I wouldn't marry couldn't be the mother of the child that I never wanted. We had to take action.

So much was going on in my life at that time. It was 2001, and I was graduating in May. I was going on job interviews. I was living at home with my mother and I had already quit the UPS Store in a leap of faith that I would get a grown-up job. I had little money in my pocket or in the bank, but I had a credit card. I approached Brittany to insist that she had to have an abortion. We weren't right for each other, and this would be a disaster. I researched and planned the entire thing, and all she had to do was go with me that day and have the procedure. "*All she had to do…*" It seemed so simple to me. Remember, I had it all figured out.

Whenever I insisted on something, Brittany didn't fight me on it. She quietly went along with the plan, knowing that the pressure didn't just come from me, but from a society that would think less of her, and from her parents, especially her Muslim father. Her father would kill her. He had already once threatened me with violence. I had to inform him that this is America and I remained armed. I dared him, saying, "Speak with actions and not words." He remained silent toward me afterward, opting instead to take his anger out on her.

In June of 2001, we scheduled the appointment for the procedure. The clinic was in midtown Atlanta. As per Georgia law at the time, it was required that she come to the clinic first, have a sonogram, and seek counseling. There was also a mandatory grace period of several days before she could have the procedure. Georgia is a red state with laws designed to discourage abortion (Guttmacher Institute, 2022). Nothing would discourage me. Not the waiting period. Not even the protesters. As we approached the clinic for the consultation, the sidewalk was lined with people holding signs calling women who chose not to have their babies murderers. So much for persuasive speeches. They were straight to the point. I wasn't worried about them getting too close to us physically. They were required by law to stay back far enough so that we could ingress and egress. But I was worried about them getting too close to her mentally.

Brittany was like an egg. She had a hard shell outside and a soft yolk inside. The day she cracked and cried that we would never get married revealed that she was breakable. We entered the clinic, went through with the consultation, scheduled the procedure for a few days later, and exited without a crack.

On the day of the procedure, I picked her up, and we headed to the clinic. There were no protesters outside on that day. We went in, I swiped my card, and she went on into the back. She was her normal self, emotionless. I was too. I had no idea what to expect. The only person I knew who had experience in this area was Mike, and he gave me few details on what happens after the procedure. What happened afterward surprised me. Brittany came out of the recovery room one hour later battered, drowsy and weak. It was as if she had been wounded in a war. Something happened in there. I didn't know what, but I knew I had to get her to a safe space where she could recover. I took her to her parents' house and dropped her off.

I checked up on Brittany frequently via phone. We even played our nightly Jeopardy competition. It seemed that she was recovering well. Physically she was okay, and mentally, she acted normal. Her follow-up appointment was in three weeks, and once that was done, the drama would be too. In just a week, Brittany and I were back to being rabbits. We probably should've waited, but we couldn't keep our hands off one another.

Three weeks passed, and we were back at the clinic. Brittany checked in at the front desk and was taken into the back for a follow-up ultrasound. I waited in the lobby. This was supposed to be a normal follow-up, but it wasn't. Brittany stormed out of the consultation room, grabbed me by the arm, and rushed me to the car. She said nothing, but her face told a story as if she had been broken again. We got in the car, and after asking her for the thousandth time what was wrong, she revealed that the ultrasound concluded that she was pregnant. "Well, they have to perform the procedure again," I said. "Obviously, they got it wrong the first time," I insisted. Frantically, she said, "No! They said this is a new pregnancy." Without hesitating, I said, "We have to get the procedure done again." But Brittany, having never shown her cards before, finally cracked. She cried as she begged, "I can't go through that again. Please No! I can't do that again."

Karla knew what I was going through. She was supportive. Our relationship continued as it had before. She steered clear of offering me advice, just a good time. Brittany pondered her next move. By August, she still hadn't made up her mind. This was back in the day when women had the right to make decisions for their own bodies. I was sweating bullets. At least I had secured a job teaching at an afterschool program for four hours a day. I had a little bit of income to pay back my credit card bill, but not enough to pay for diapers. Still, I hadn't learned my lesson.

Dinner was followed by dessert in the bedroom. Karla and I found ourselves wrapped up in a familiar sexual exchange that we had been carrying out for countless months. On this particular, steamy late July evening we were extra, extra wild. As always, I checked the condom periodically to ensure that it was still in place and that it wasn't at risk of breaking. Karla and I had broken condoms before, but we simply stopped and replaced them. Aside from changing them out every 30 minutes or so, I was still Quick Withdraw McGraw, making sure to pull out every time, even though we were shielded. But something was different this go-round. As I neared climax, I worried that the condom was coming off. I couldn't hold back. As I ejaculated, I simultaneously pulled out, leaving the condom deep inside of her. I knew I was in trouble. I felt it. My men were marching toward the fortress and were sure to breach the front gate. My spidey sense was once again ringing.

Late in August, Karla called me and said these words, "I'm pregnant, but don't worry, I am having an abortion. I spoke to my mom, and she's coming down to Atlanta the day of the procedure. All you need to do is give me half the money." It was official at that moment: I had two women pregnant at the same time. I was a dirty dude living a soap opera life.

Just as I had with Brittany, I took Karla to her initial consultation. She got her ultrasound and her date was scheduled for a week later. She was fine with it, and the experience with her was less stressful than the other situation I was navigating. She even asked me how that was going. The night before the procedure, her mother took the bus into town to support us. In stark contrast to Brittany's dad, she was so cool and kind. We even had a candid conversation about how it happened. On the day of the procedure, we all went to the clinic. I gave my half of the money; Karla went to the back, had the abortion, and came out as if nothing had ever happened. She walked out of the clinic as if she had just had her teeth cleaned. That evening, her mother got back on the bus and returned to her hometown. The End. But it wasn't the end.

Two days later, I got a frantic call from Karla's roommate telling me to get there as soon as possible. Karla was experiencing extreme pain and was bleeding heavily. I could hear Karla in the background screaming at the top of her lungs. I rushed over there, and by the time I arrived, she had already been loaded into the back of an ambulance. I followed them to a nearby hospital, parked, and waited until they placed her in a room. What the hell was going on?

Karla was placed in a room and hooked up to a ton of machines. They shot her up with the painkillers, but I could've used some too. I had been in the delivery room right before Mike's son was born. I recognized this setting. They were monitoring Karla to see what had happened with her procedure. One of the machines was an ultrasound monitor, and one of the sounds I heard was a loud and rapid thumping. I knew that sound. It was the sound of trouble. It was the heartbeat of our baby. The doctor came into the room and confirmed my worst fears.

Karla burst into a panic. She was angry, scared, and confused. She questioned how this could happen. The hospital doctor offered no answers. He simply said to her, "You are still pregnant. You should go back to the clinic and speak with the clinician," and left. This had to be a cruel joke. I couldn't possibly dream up something so out of left field. Karla began thinking that maybe this was a sign from God that she needed to keep the baby. I went into full crisis mode. I had to steer this sinking ship in the right direction. We needed to head back to '*sure*,' but Karla was drifting deeper and deeper into murky waters. The next few days would be hell, but I finally convinced her that we needed to return to the clinic to find out what happened. She agreed, but she wanted accountability. I wanted opportunity. I wanted a chance to convince her to have the abortion again.

On September 6, 2001, I was negotiating with two women I had impregnated, neither of which wanted to go through their abortion ordeals again. Brittany had made an appointment with her doctor for the following Tuesday. Meanwhile, Karla and I went back to the clinic that botched her procedure a week prior. We arrived at the clinic late in the afternoon. Karla and I were the last ones on the schedule to consult with the doctor who performed the procedure. It started off rocky. He entered the room, and she instantly went off on him, screaming like a crazy person and threatening to sue him. Her words were a hot bowl of fury, fire, and confusion. I was the voice of reason, and the doctor and I both sought to lower her tone.

The doctor and I were on the same team. He didn't want to be sued, and I didn't want to be a dad. We managed to quiet her down long enough for him to explain that what she experienced is known as a "missed abortion" and happens in about 1 in 200 cases. He explained that he would take extra care this time to ensure that her procedure was successful. After about an hour in his office, she agreed to have the procedure again. He agreed to perform it immediately. He instructed her to go to the operating room, remove her clothes, and wait for him. She did.

The doctor and I had been friendly up until that moment. At one point, we even realized that he knew my grandfather growing up in Jamaica. He talked about how well respected my grandfather was. I laughed it up with him, but I realized that I was following in my grandfather's footsteps. My grandfather's legacy was that of traveling the island, impregnating women, and not taking responsibility for the kids. How ironic that the abortion doctor bragged about knowing a guy known for how many children he created and didn't support.

When Karla went into the procedure room, the friendliness between the doctor and me evaporated. I didn't have to be Mr. Nice Guy anymore. Desperation had overtaken me. I leaned over the table, looked him in the eye, and threatened him. I told him, "YOU ARE FUCKING WITH MY LIFE! YOU ARE GONNA GET THIS SHIT RIGHT THIS TIME! DO YOU UNDERSTAND ME?" Heeding my threat, the doctor assured me I would not be disappointed. He exited the office and went back into the procedure room.

One hour later, Karla came out, battered. It was a very different scene from the first procedure when she exited the procedure seemingly unscathed. The doctor gave me a list of care instructions and let me know, "It is done." I took Karla home and stayed with her for the next few hours until she encouraged me to go home.

Now, I was down to just one pregnant woman.

Brittany's appointment was scheduled to take place early morning on September 11. She drove herself that morning to the doctor. I stayed home, watching the iconic towers that I once marveled at being attacked and destroyed. It was all bad news. I cried that morning. Telephone service across the nation was jammed, and reaching family and friends back home in New York was impossible. As I mourned the loss of two buildings and thousands of lives, Brittany called me to discuss her doctor's visit. Her doctor didn't believe that she was still pregnant. Ordinarily, I would've celebrated, but the shock of what was happening in the world was too much for me to register any joy. A week later, Brittany and I returned to the abortion clinic, where she took another ultrasound exam. It was confirmed. The clinic believed that her immune system rejected the fetus and that she had a miscarriage.

My relationship with Brittany continued for another two years. After four and a half years and three pregnancies, I decided that it was better to move on with our lives. I lost contact with Brittany shortly after that, but in 2010 she reached out to me via phone. My number hadn't changed, and neither had she. She reported to me that she was married with a daughter and that her husband had caught her cheating with a local politician. That was our last conversation.

Karla and I remained friends for years and continued our sexual relationship until 2012. We took breaks whenever either one of us was in a relationship. I was in a very serious relationship for nearly six years, and she had a relationship with her children's father for a while, but in 2010 we resumed occasional relations.

I never took a deep sigh of relief after those crazy moments. My actions may have been cold, but like Brittany, I had a hard exterior and an egg yolk inside my shell. I felt guilty for what I did but justified it as what needed to be done. Life tested me, and I can't honestly say that I passed. I just got through it.

I regret my irresponsibility. I regret the hurt I caused those women and even the hurt I caused myself. I will probably never see Brittany again. Karla and I haven't spoken in many years, and I can't go backward to ask them for forgiveness, but I can forgive myself. I have forgiven myself. I have healed myself and marched forward without my soldiers.

From here on, I'm having fun. Responsible fun.

Writing this book has been one of the great accomplishments of my life, but it's one of many. If you've enjoyed this project please visit my merch store at www.ChildFreeAndHavingFun.com.

Also, order a copy of my childrens' book entitled "Dana the Procrastinator" at www.KidsReid.com.

And lastly, and certainly not least, voiceover has been the love of my life since 2004 and I've voiced and produced countless projects. Take a listen to my work at www.DaneReidMedia.com.

References

All About the Students (2021, October 26). *How much does a university degree cost in Venezuela?* Todo sobre el alumnado. https://unate.org/en/instituciones-educativas/cuanto-cuesta-una-carrera-universitaria-en-venezuela.html

Aloi, D. (2005). *Mothers face disadvantages in getting hired, Cornell study says.* Cornell Chronicle. https://news.cornell.edu/stories/2005/08/mothers-face-disadvantages-getting-hired-study-shows

Amber, J. (2020, October 27). *In her own words: Marissa Alexander tells her story.* Essence. https://www.essence.com/news/marissa-alexander-exclusive/

American Foundation for Suicide Prevention. (2022, June 14). *Suicide statistics.* https://afsp.org/suicide-statistics/#:~:text=Additional%20facts%20about%20suicide%20in%20the%20US&text=On%20average%2C%20there%20are%20130,of%20suicide%20deaths%20in%202020

Aminu, R. T. (2017). Redefining Best Interest of the Child: The Crushing Impact of Child Support Debts on Low-Income Families in the Minority Communities. *T. Marshall L. Rev.*, *43*, 561.

Anderson, D. M., & Sabia, J. J. (2018). Child-access-prevention laws, youths' gun carrying, and school shootings. *The Journal of Law and Economics*, *61*(3), 489-524. https://doi.org/10.1086/699657

Austin, M. W. (2016). *Conceptions of parenthood: Ethics and the family.* Routledge.

Blackmon, M. (2022, February 11). *Condomless sex is on the rise. This is why some people don't use them anymore.* BuzzFeed News. https://www.buzzfeednews.com/article/michaelblackmon/why-people-arent-using-condoms

Bloomgarden-Smoke, K. (2015, August 13). *Home on the (Free) range: How Lenore Skenazy turned a column into a movement.* Observer. https://observer.com/2015/08/lenore-skenazy-free-range-kids/

Blunk, S. S., Clark, D. E., & McGibany, J. M. (2006). Evaluating the long-run impacts of the 9/11 terrorist attacks on US domestic airline travel. *Applied economics*, *38*(4), 363-370. https://doi.org/10.1080/00036840500367930

Bouchrika, I. (2021). What Is Included in Room and Board in College: How to Cover the Costs?

Bradford, S. (2010, June 1). *Raising children costs between $286,000 and $476,000.* CBS News - Breaking news, 24/7 live streaming news & top stories. https://www.cbsnews.com/news/raising-children-costs-between-286000-and-476000/

Brehm, E., & Flaws, J. A. (2019). Transgenerational effects of endocrine-disrupting chemicals on male and female reproduction. *Endocrinology*, *160*(6), 1421-1435. https://doi.org/10.1210/en.2019-00034

Burchel, B. (2017). How will Millennials invest differently than their parents?

Carroll, L. (2019, May 11). *Chickenpox is a lifelong herpes virus that comes with a serious side effect.* NBC News. https://www.nbcnews.com/health/kids-health/chickenpox-lifelong-herpes-virus-comes-serious-side-effect-n1004201

Centers for Disease Control (CDC). (2020, May 14). *Depression among women.* Centers for Disease Control and Prevention. https://www.cdc.gov/reproductivehealth/depression/index.htm#Postpartum

Centers for Disease Control. (2015, November 6). *Gestational weight gain — United States, 2012 and 2013.* Centers for Disease Control and Prevention. https://www.cdc.gov/mmwr/preview/mmwrhtml/mm6443a3.htm?s_cid=mm6443a3_w

Chowdhury, R. B., Moore, G. A., Weatherley, A. J., & Arora, M. (2017). Key sustainability challenges for the global phosphorus resource, their implications for global food security, and options for mitigation. *Journal of Cleaner Production*, *140*, 945-963. https://doi.org/10.1016/j.jclepro.2016.07.012

Crittenden, P. M. (1988). Relationships at risk. *Clinical implications of attachment*, 136-174.

Crowley, J. E. (2008). Defiant dads: Fathers' rights activists in America. Cornell University Press.

DeWeerdt, S. (2017, December 15). The Washington Post. https://www.washingtonpost.com/national/health-science/the-link-between-autism-and-older-parents-is-clear-but-the-why-is-not/2017/12/15/dbe03284-dc62-11e7-b859-fb0995360725_story.html

Dickson, EJ. (2019, December 13). My wife's postpartum body is different. I don't know what to do. *Fatherly.* *https://www.fatherly.com/love-money/wife-postpartum-body-not-attracted*

Dorrien, G. J. (2018). *Breaking white supremacy: Martin Luther King Jr. and the black social gospel.* Yale University Press.

Dworkin-McDaniel, N. (2017, November 17). Why women stay with men who cheat. *Everyday Health.* https://www.everydayhealth.com/healthy-living/why-women-stay-with-men-who-cheat/

Emmott, S. (2021, August 25). *Humans – the real threat to life on earth.* The Guardian. https://www.theguardian.com/environment/2013/jun/30/stephen-emmott-ten-billion

Feiner, L. (2021). *Facebook whistleblower: The company knows it's harming people and the buck stops with Zuckerberg.* CNBC. https://www.cnbc.com/2021/10/05/facebook-whistleblower-testifies-before-senate-committee.html

Ferrara, M. M. (2009). Broadening the Myopic Vision of Parent Involvement. *School Community Journal, 19*(2), 123-142.

Gabbat, A. (2018, November 5). *Spanking children makes them more aggressive, US pediatricians' body says*. The Guardian. https://www.theguardian.com/us-news/2018/nov/05/spanking-children-makes-them-more-aggressive-us-pediatricians-body-says

Gaugler, J. E. (2005). Family involvement in residential long-term care: A synthesis and critical review. *Aging & mental health*, *9*(2), 105-118. https://doi.org/10.10 80%2F13607860412331310245

Greer, J. (2022, April 18). *Family legacies: Why should we care?* Focus on the Family. https://www.focusonthefamily.com/parenting/family-legacies/

Gunderman, R. (2019, September 6). *Dr. Spock's timeless lessons in parenting*. The Conversation. https://theconversation.com/dr-spocks-timeless-lessons-in-parenting-122377

Guttmacher Institute (2022, June 28). State facts about abortion: Georgia. https://www.guttmacher.org/fact-sheet/state-facts-about-abortion-georgia

Hamilton, D., Lemeshow, S., Saleska, J. L., Brewer, B., & Strobino, K. (2018). Who owns guns and how do they keep them? The influence of household characteristics on firearms ownership and storage practices in the United States. *Preventive medicine*, *116*, 134-142. https://doi.org/10.1016/j.ypmed.2018.07.013

Hess, A. J. (2019). *It costs almost $80,000 to go to the most expensive college in the US—but here's how much students actually pay*. CNBC. https://www.cnbc.com/2019/08/11/it-costs-almost-80000-to-go-to-the-most-expensive-college-in-the-us.html

https://research.com/education/what-is-included-in-room-and-board-in-college

Hutson, R. (2007, April 4). *Child support and parental conflict in low-income families*. Children and Youth Services Review. 29(9), 1142-1157. doi: 10.1016/JChildYouth.2007.04.004 https://www.researchgate.net/publication/4825252_Child_support_and_parental_conflict_in_low-income_families

Jordan, A. (2021, August 17). *Productivity hit by parents caring for ill children.* Small Business UK. https://smallbusiness.co.uk/productivity-hit-by-parents-caring-for-ill-children-2498401/

Kramer, S. (2019). US has world's highest rate of children living in single-parent households. https://policycommons.net/artifacts/616475/us/1597144/

Laponsie, M. (2021, September 17). How Much Does It Cost to Raise a Child? U.S. News. https://money.usnews.com/money/personal-finance/articles/how-much-does-it-cost-to-raise-a-child/

Learish, J. (2020, June 3). *The cost of giving birth in each state.* CBS News - Breaking news, 24/7 live streaming news & top stories. https://www.cbsnews.com/pictures/cost-giving-birth-in-united-states/

Lee, A. (2014). *Common core state standards.* Understood - For learning and thinking differences. https://www.understood.org/en/articles/common-core-state-standards-what-you-need-to-know

Li, D. K. (2013, November 8). *Man sues wife after she gives him 'ugly' baby.* New York Post. https://nypost.com/2013/11/07/wife-must-pay-120k-for-disclosing-plastic-surgeries/

Luke-Norris. (2020, April 22). *How Charles Barkley's controversial 'I am not a role model' Nike spot came to be.* Sportscasting | Pure Sports. https://www.sportscasting.com/how-charles-barkleys-controversial-i-am-not-a-role-model-nike-spot-came-to-be/

MacKinnon, E. (2022, January 26). *Is there an age limit to male fertility?* livescience.com. https://www.livescience.com/24196-male-fertility-limit.html

Mane, G., & Maid, S. (2021). Contraception in adolescents. *Health Strategies and Interventions in Adolescents for Future Reproductive Health*, 60.

Marsh, M., & Ronner, W. (2008). *The fertility doctor: John Rock and the reproductive revolution.* JHU Press.

Martin, J., Kane, S. V., & Feagins, L. A. (2016). Fertility and contraception in women with inflammatory bowel disease. *Gastroenterology & Hepatology*, *12*(2), 101. https://pubmed.ncbi.nlm.nih.gov/27182211

Maunz, M. E. (n.d.). *Why your child's brain is like a sponge*. Age of Montessori. https://ageofmontessori.org/why-your-childs-brain-is-like-a-sponge/

Mehdi, S. (2021, August 9). *"I am not paid to be a role model": When Charles Barkley controversially claimed to not want to emulate a parent-like demeanor in an advert for Nike*. The SportsRush. https://thesportsrush.com/nba-news-i-am-not-paid-to-be-a-role-model-when-charles-barkley-controversially-claimed-to-not-want-to-emulate-a-parent-like-demeanor-in-an-advert-for-nike/

Miller, C. C. (2019, March 26). *The relentlessness of modern parenting (Published 2018)*. The New York Times - Breaking News, US News, World News and Videos. https://www.nytimes.com/2018/12/25/upshot/the-relentlessness-of-modern-parenting.html

Morrison-Williams, S. (2022). Millennials - Millennials- Changing the face of higher education. https://educationinitiative.thepacificinstitute.com/articles/story/millennials-changing-the-face-of-higher-education1

Office for National Statistics (ONS). (2019, October 23). *Families and the labour market, UK*. Home - Office for National Statistics. https://www.ons.gov.uk/employmentandlabourmarket/peopleinwork/employmentandemployeetypes/articles/familiesandthelabourmarketengland/2019

Orlando, J. (2012). *Penalties for illegal handgun possession*. C G A. https://www.cga.ct.gov/2012/rpt/2012-R-0345.htm

Paid Sick Time. (2018, September 10). *Back to school: Working parents, know your rights when your child is sick*. A Better Balance. https://www.abetterbalance.org/back-to-school-working-parents-know-your-rights-when-your-child-is-sick/

Palmer, G. (2012, June 25). *More U.S. teens hide online activity from parents - survey*. U.S. https://www.reuters.com/article/online-teens-idUSL2E8HPDSA20120625

Paul, K., & Milmo, D. (2021, October 4). *Facebook putting profit before public good, says whistleblower Frances Haugen.* The Guardian. https://www.theguardian. com/technology/2021/oct/03/former-facebook-employee-frances-haugen-identifies-herself-as-whistleblower

Petersen, A. H. (2021, August 26). *Caring for the elderly has never been more expensive, exhausting, or invisible.* Vox. https://www.vox.com/the-goods/22639674/elder-care-family-costs-nursing-home-health-care

Pilkington, E. (2017, November 26). *Tyler Clementi, student outed as gay on internet, jumps to his death.* The Guardian. https://www.theguardian.com/world/2010/sep/30/tyler-clementi-gay-student-suicide

Powell, C. S. (2017, December 20). *How humans might outlive earth, the sun...and even the universe.* NBC News. https://www.nbcnews.com/mach/science/how-humans-might-outlive-earth-sun-even-universe-ncna831291

Rankin, J. A., Paisley, C. A., Tomeny, T. S., & Eldred, S. W. (2019). Fathers of youth with autism spectrum disorder: A systematic review of the impact of fathers' involvement on youth, families, and intervention. *Clinical Child and Family Psychology Review, 22*(4), 458-477. https://doi.org/10.1007/s10567-019-00294-0

Rathore, R. (2021, April 13). *Tough times create strong men, strong men create easy times. Easy times create weak men, weak men create tough times.* LinkedIn. https://www.linkedin.com/pulse/tough-times-create-strong-men-easy-weak-rishabh-rathoresmith

Rebecca, E. (2016, May 25). *From tiger to free-range parents – what research says about pros and cons of popular parenting styles.* The Conversation. https://theconversation.com/from-tiger-to-free-range-parents-what-research-says-about-pros-and-cons-of-popular-parenting-styles-57986

Sandin, S., Lichtenstein, P., Kuja-Halkola, R., Larsson, H., Hultman, C. M., & Reichenberg, A. (2014). The familial risk of autism. *Jama, 311*(17), 1770-1777. https://doi.org/10.1001/jama.2014.4144

Smith, K. A. (2021, October 21). *3 warning signs of financial abuse—And how victims can recover*. Forbes Advisor. https://www.forbes.com/advisor/personal-finance/signs-of-financial-abuse-domestic-violence-awareness/

Smithers, R. (2017, September 20). *Who sends their sick child to school?* The Guardian. https://www.theguardian.com/education/mortarboard/2010/sep/08/sick-children-sent-to-school

Songfacts. (n.d.). *Lyrics for Izzo (H.O.V.A.) by Jay-Z - Songfacts*. 400 Good Request. https://www.songfacts.com/lyrics/jay-z/izzo-hova

Steber, C. (2018, February 21). *These 12 bad habits are really easy to inherit from your parents*. Bustle. https://www.bustle.com/p/these-12-bad-habits-are-really-easy-to-inherit-from-your-parents-8230645

Tomaswick, A. (2021, October 17). *This'll be us... in 5 billion years*. Universe Today. https://www.universetoday.com/152996/thisll-be-us-in-5-billion-years/#:~:text=Scientists%20have%20long%20known%20the,to%20the%20orbit%20of%20Mars

Villines, Z. (2020). *Having a baby at 40: Benefits and risks*. Medical and health information. https://www.medicalnewstoday.com/articles/having-a-baby-at-40

Villines, Z. (2020, January 10). What is the best age to have a baby? *Medical News Today*. https://www.medicalnewstoday.com/articles/best-age-to-have-a-baby

Watts, S. (2018, September 17). *Why do some serial killers turn into cannibals?* A&E. https://www.aetv.com/real-crime/cannibal-serial-killers-jeffrey-dahmer-albert-fish-andrei-chikatilo-psychology-of-cannibalism

Wolff-Mann, E. (2020, July 14). The 2008 recession was far worse for young people's careers than previously thought. Yahoo Finance - Stock Market Live, Quotes, Business & Finance News. https://finance.yahoo.com/news/the-2008-recession-was-far-worse-for-young-peoples-careers-than-previously-thought-200751863.html?guccounter=1&guce_referrer=aHR0cHM6Ly93d3cuZ29vZ2xlLmNvbS8&guce_referrer_sig=AQAAAKNI3sbWsWCf44BJ4iLT3hRCnoYkk--1SDCtMefILooRPmuqbGJpNKyXnHvqXdq-PoCxZ5s-mZofJa-pGIXrRDeHRMtSIZWZpO8jJIW2-unb_y0a1UWwORnlwvbHGnG7-viaFK7HJ81mKhH-62YFGV__0lywbAV6RMuLbxwUxcGd

World Health Organization. (2019, September 19). *Maternal mortality.* https://www.who.int/news-room/fact-sheets/detail/maternal-mortality